Enterprise and the Scope of the Firm

Enterprise and the Scope of the Firm

The role of vertical integration

MORRIS SILVER

Martin Robertson

© Morris Silver, 1984

First published in 1984
by Martin Robertson & Company Ltd.,
108 Cowley Road, Oxford OX4 1JF.

All rights reserved. Except for the quotation of short
passages for the purpose of criticism and review, no part
of this publication may be reproduced, stored in
a retrieval system, or transmitted, in any form or by
any means, electronic, mechanical, photocopying,
recording or otherwise, without the prior written
permission of the copyright holder.

British Library Cataloguing in Publication Data
Silver, Morris
   Enterprise and the scope of the firm.
   1. Technological innovations   2. Management
   I. Title
   658.4'063   HD45

ISBN 0-85520-737-X

Typeset by Cambrian Typesetters,
Aldershot, Hants.
Printed and bound in Great Britain by
Billing and Sons Ltd, Worcester

Contents

Preface and Acknowledgements   xi

1   Entrepreneurship: An Introductory Perspective   1

PART I   INNOVATION, INFORMATION IMPACTEDNESS AND VERTICAL INTEGRATION

2   Vertical Integration and the Employer–Employee Relationship   11

3   Mergers and Economic Change   20

4   The Onset of Vertical Integration   23
    4.1 Case Studies from American Business History
    4.2 Case Studies from Other Parts of the World
    4.3 Case Studies of Early Industrialization in Backward Areas
    4.4 Case Studies on the Roles of Merchants and Landowners

5   A Model of Vertical Integration and Disintegration with Supporting Evidence   44
    5.1 The Cost-Minimizing Extent of Vertical Integration
    5.2 The Contributions of Managerial and Organizational Innovations and Technological Change
    5.3 Vertical Integration and the Passage of Time
    5.4 Vertical Integration and 'Quiet Times'
    5.5 The Tenacity of the Expertise Factor
    5.6 Original Innovators Compared with New Entrants
    5.7 An Econometric Challenge
    5.8 Case Study Evidence
    5.9 Marxist Perspectives on Vertical Integration
    5.10 The Alleged Modernity of Vertical Integration

PART II APPLICATIONS OF THE MODEL OF VERTICAL INTEGRATION AND DISINTEGRATION TO MAJOR THEMES IN ECONOMIC HISTORY

6 On Imperialist Enclaves and Dependency 71
   6.1 Penetration by Foreign Firms, The Example of Sugar
   6.2 Legal Restrictions and Contractual Substitutes for Vertical Integration
   6.3 The Emergence and Retreat of Enclaves
   6.4 Concluding Remarks

7 The Rises and Falls of Manors, Latifundia and Bonanzas 80
   7.1 Medieval England
   7.2 Organizational Trends in Greco-Roman Agriculture
   7.3 The 'Second Serfdom' in Germany and Poland
   7.4 The Experience of the US: Plantations in the South, Bonanzas and Cattle Kings in the West
   7.5 Concluding Remarks

8 The Putting-Out System and the Development of Capitalism 98

PART III COMPETING AND COMPLEMENTARY EXPLANATIONS OF VERTICAL INTEGRATION

9 Vertical Integration as a Defense Against Opportunistic Recontracting 107

10 Vertical Integration to Control Input Quality 112

11 Vertical Integration Induced by Government Policies 115
   11.1 Market Economies
   11.2 Centrally Planned Economies

12 Monopolization as a Motive for Vertical Integration 122
   12.1 The Portland Cement-Ready Mix Concrete Merger Wave
   12.2 The Aluminum Industry
   12.3 The Petroleum Industry

13 Market Size Limitations on the Division of Labor and Vertical Integration 131
   13.1 The Onset of Vertical Integration

    13.2 Historical Evidence
    13.3 Vertical Disintegration
    13.4 Econometric Evidence

Concluding Remarks   138
Appendix 1   139
Appendix 2   147
References   156
Index   183

To Lilly and Tillie

Preface and Acknowledgements

This study proposes an explanation of vertical integration and disintegration in terms of entrepreneurial innovation and the consequent rise and fall of information transmission costs. In judging the validity of this hypothesis several formal statistical tests are considered, but primary reliance is placed on case studies. Given the breadth of my subject, I trust that I will be forgiven for relying so heavily on secondary sources. I have striven to be cautious, critical, and objective in selecting the 'authorities' on whom I am forced to rely. The case study approach is, of course, a well-established method of writing about business history. I believe that the business historian will take pleasure in seeing his case studies used to lend concreteness to general economic principles. I also believe that the economist will appreciate the value of case studies when, as is undoubtedly the case with respect to vertical integration, econometric procedures are very different to apply. Relatively little empirical research has been devoted to the determinants of vertical integration. Indeed, it is not an easy task to design a conceptually sound quantitative measure of entrepreneurial innovation that would be valid across firms and industries or over time. To the best of my knowledge no such measure has been devised.

Another point which should not be ignored is that econometric studies are not always so very different from case studies as we would like to believe. How many experimental regressions utilizing different combinations of variables, forms, and approaches lie unseen behind each neat equation on the page of a journal? The published result may well be a 'case study'. To employ the language of statistical testing the probability of incorrectly rejecting the null hypothesis (Type I error) is, to an unknown degree, greater than the purported level of significance. The emperor does have new clothes but they are not so grand.

Nevertheless, when all is said and done, the fact remains that case studies no matter how diverse or appropriately chosen do not constitute a rigorous test. The case study approach helps the scholar to see whether a proposed explanation clashes with the most obvious facts. This is only the first stage of testing, but for most questions it is as far as we shall be able to go. The present essay is then an initial report on what must inevitably be a very long-term project. It will have served its purpose if it helps to shape a new intellectual climate in which theories, evidence, and policy recommendations about vertical integration are refined and sharpened.

For their helpful comments and suggestions I would like to express my gratitude to Armen A. Alchian, Alfred D. Chandler Jr, Malcolm Galatin, Robert Higgs, Mitchell Kellman, Israel M. Kirzner, George Sawyer, Gordon Tullock and, especially, to two anonymous referees of this Press. The responsibility for any errors is mine alone. My research was greatly facilitated by a grant from a fund created by the will of the late Harry Schwager, a distinguished alumnus of the City College of New York, class of 1911. My wife Sondra and our two sons Gerry and Ron made the most precious contribution of all, peace of mind.

CHAPTER 1

Entrepreneurship: An Introductory Perspective

The entrepreneur produces new economic ideas (new information) and gains control over the productive inputs necessary to implement them.[1] His activity, as Kirzner (1977, pp. 157, 172) notes, involves 'breaking away from the ignorance that previously prevailed [in the market]' and reflects not only the primordial desire for gain, but 'the tendency for purposeful human beings to become aware of available opportunities'. Buchanan and Di Pierro (1980, p. 699) who refer to the modern Austrian theory of entrepreneurship remark that: 'The paradigm for entrepreneurial choice becomes economic arbitrage, rather than the balls-and-urns probabilistic calculus. ... Profit-seeking entrepreneurs create their own cross-input, cross-technology, cross-output, cross-domain relationships which offer potential gains to all parties and which do not come into being, do not exist, without entrepreneurial action.' Within this kind of perspective, they conclude, it may not be possible to model entrepreneurial choice in a manner that the formal decision theorist would find satisfying.

Nevertheless, as Schumpeter (1934, p. 68) forcefully argued, entrepreneurship is the mainspring of economic development. More recently, Casson (1982, p. 14) has explained that:

The entrepreneur believes that he is right, while everyone else is wrong. Thus the essence of entrepreneurship is being different – being different because one has a different perception of the situation. It is this that makes the entrepreneur so important. Were he not present, things would have been done very differently.

A striking contrast in approach is provided by Marx who, while recognizing the prodevelopment character of 'capitalism', at least in its early stages, portrayed this as the inevitable result of the interplay of the 'forces and relations of production'. Operating at this level of abstraction, Marx was able to ignore and even denigrate entrepreneurship, thus projecting the vision of a surrealistic world in which there is progress without progressives. Indeed, it is shown in appendix 1 that the cornerstone of Marxian economics, the theory of the exploitation of labor, rests in the final analysis on the largely implicit assumption that entrepreneurial innovation is unimportant if not non-existent.[2]

The opportunity to produce a specific, economically valuable, new idea may be widely distributed in the society with profit opportunities for those who first search, see, and implement. Alternatively, it may be specialized in terms of the individual's prior education and experience (Mighell and Jones 1963, p. 29). Typically, Malmgren (1961, p. 413) notes, 'when new opportunities, or *market vacua* ... appear the uneven distribution of initially required information and the faulty communication of the new information enables one or more firms to enter the *vacua* while others do not'. In practice, the innovator is usually a merchant, larger producer, or traveled individual who has acquired some familiarity with production for markets. In communication terminology one might say that roles of this kind provide the actor with an *information channel* and the requisite *code*, or technical vocabulary. The economist would say that such roles provide the actor with a comparative advantage in innovation – that is, relatively low opportunity costs of searching for and implementing new economic ideas. In addition, individuals with such a background often have personal or family wealth, contacts, and other attributes which provide them with better than average access to the capital necessary to act upon their insights.[3]

In colonial North America, for example, those who became manufacturers were almost invariably merchants who saw profit opportunities in diversifying their economic activities (E.J. Perkins 1980, p. 93). Later, during the seminal 1870s, the typical American industrial leader came from an urban, business-oriented family (Gregory and Neu 1952, p. 204). Indeed, taking the entire period from 1865 to 1925, the steel industry obtained nearly 90 per cent of its leaders from business, landed, or professional families (Erickson 1959, pp. 11–12). Also during the 1870s and 1880s, experienced midwestern stockmen pioneered the development of western ranch properties (Bogue 1963, pp. 99–100). Crossing the Atlantic a similar pattern is evident. During the 1834 to 1879 period, the pioneering Rhineland entrepreneurs were sons of physicians, of teachers, and especially, of clergymen (Schmitt 1975, p. 69). Kocka (1978, p. 532) adds the important point that:

Up to 1870, almost every third entrepreneur in the Rhineland and Westphalia had been on business or study visits abroad. . . . The 'Grand Tour,' which was common in the aristocracy, meant that many Silesian magnates became acquainted with English methods. . . . The long educational stay with foreign business friends and the frequent business trips abroad were long standing practices of the larger merchant.

Further, many famous West German entrepreneurs of the industrial revolution came from prominent families, which had for a long time been active in industrial and business pursuits (Kocka 1978, p. 510). Similarly, in the nineteenth century the mechanized production of textiles was introduced into the rural areas of the Zurich canton by rural tradesmen, rural dealers, and rural craftsmen who had been trained in the putting-out (or domestic) system (Braun 1967, p. 557).

These prerequisites for entrepreneurial success apply also to the Third World. Thus, a stratified random sample of 250 Muslim entrepreneurs in Pakistan (Papenek 1962, pp. 52–3) revealed that, in the late 1950s:

Persons whose primary occupation before 1947 (or before entering trade, if this was later) was trade furnished almost half the entrepreneurs for Pakistan's industry. They set up the larger or more rapidly growing firms and now control nearly 70 percent of capital. . . . A large proportion of all entrepreneurs had fathers and grandfathers in trade. Trading was their traditional occupation and a change to industry was an entrepreneurial decision.

In sharp contrast to this, only 3 per cent of the industrialists had agriculture as their previous primary occupation. Again, in today's Zambia most of the leading African businessmen had fathers who were primarily employed in the cash economy (Beveridge and Oberschall 1979, pp. 129–30). Patterns similar to those observed in Pakistan and Zambia have also been found in India, the Philippines, Nigeria, Lebanon, and Greece (Nafziger 1978, pp. 27–31, 123–9).

The importance of a cosmopolitan background in future entrepreneurial success is well illustrated by the British firm, Imperial Chemical Industries, which was founded by the German Jew, Ludwig Mond, and the American company set up by the Irishman turned Peruvian, W.R. Grace. Both of these firms may quite properly be described as having been 'born multinational'.[4] A final example of some interest is provided by the evolution of Royal Dutch Shell (Holland/UK). This firm began in 1833 as a London shop selling, among other things, oriental shells. Before very long the shells were being shipped directly. Then, building on this information base, Marcus Samuels and his son developed step by step, a general import and export business, imported kerosene, purchased tankers to transport oil and went on to establish oil storage facilities in the Far East (Buckley and Roberts 1982, p. 94).

A new dimension of insight into the sources of innovative behavior is provided by Vernon's observation (1966, pp. 191–2) that, since 'producers in any market are more likely to be aware of the possibility of introducing new products in that market than producers located elsewhere would be', American firms would generally be the first 'to offer a new product responsive to wants at higher levels of income'.[5] This hypothesis stressing comparative advantage in information collection is quite consistent with information theory which recognizes that, based upon his accumulated experience or environment, an individual may find it easier and cheaper to open certain information channels than others. Earlier, of course, beginning mainly in the second half of the seventeenth century, the role of introducing income elastic new products had been played by English entrepreneurs.[6] In the 1770s, for example, they led the way from the older, heavier woollens, to lighter, brighter worsteds demanded by the rising urban middle-class at home and on the Continent (C. Wilson 1957,

p. 106). But if those in a market are more likely to introduce new products for that market, why were so many successful businessmen in the new automobile industry of the US drawn from the ranks of bicycle manufacturers, rather than from the long-established transportation equipment industry? (Rae 1959, pp. 8–19). The explanation seems to be that, despite appearances, the former were actually 'in the market' while the latter were not; the bicycle boom of the 1890s served to make the leaders of this industry aware of the desire of consumers for a light personal transportation vehicle (Abernathy 1978, pp. 11–12; Rosenberg 1963, pp. 434–6).

The argument and evidence put forward by Higgs (1971, and 1980) that urbanization stimulates inventive or entrepreneurial activity can be viewed as an important application of Vernon's insight concerning the informational advantages of being in the market.

In the absence of mass communications systems, the average search cost of information about potential markets for inventions was an increasing function of market distance; therefore, the market as perceived by a potential investor was largely restricted to nearby locations. Assuming that the locational distribution of actual inventive opportunities coincided with that of the population, the probability that an opportunity would be perceived was then much higher for urban than for rural people. (1971, p. 662)

Emphasis upon spatial differences in possession of the requisite information channels and codes may also deepen our understanding of the emergence of specialized industrial regions, i.e. of the location problem. The fruitfulness of this approach is well illustrated by F.E. Ian Hamilton's (1974, p. 10) discussion of the experience of Lancashire in the industrial revolution.

In other words, it is neither sufficient nor correct to argue that Lancashire in England became a specialized cotton textile manufacturing region because of its comparative advantages in that industry. The contact patterns of potential entrepreneurs living in the region (landowners, traders, handicraftsmen) with merchants in Liverpool who began to handle American cotton encouraged many to start cotton-spinning or weaving as their initial industrial activity, perhaps substituting the use of cotton for the traditional commodity, wool. Locally, in each area, would-be entrepreneurs might imitate the apparently successful first few cotton textile manufacturers.

Hamilton (p. 11) adds that the isolation of Lancashire, the paucity of its contacts with other types of entrepreneurs and products operated to preclude greater intra-regional industrial diversification.

Whatever his social or industrial origins, the entrepreneur is always, to adopt Leibenstein's (1968) phrase, a 'gap-filler', or in Kirzner's (1973), an 'arbitrager'. But as Schumpeter (1934, pp. 86–7) correctly warned, the economic environment is not passive, it reacts against those seeking to do new things. The central theme of the present study is that, when wielded by the innovator, *vertical integration* (see chapter 2) is a powerful weapon for dominating and reshaping a stubborn economic fabric. It is argued that vertical integration facilitates the implementation of new ideas by reducing information transmission costs. This thesis draws together and illumines a large body of evidence from business history pertaining to the onset of vertical integration. Next the argument is extended to demonstrate that, as a new industry ages, the cost-minimizing extent of vertical integration will tend to decline. The model accounts not only for vertical mergers to cope with market bottlenecks but with 'dismergers', or the breaking-up of firms. After a longer or shorter period, Alfred Chandler's (1977) 'visible hand' tends to recede into the background if not into invisibility.

As Kaserman (1978, p. 483) concludes in his recent survey: 'Over time, as the literature in this area has evolved, there has been no discernible convergence of opinion regarding the dominant incentives for . . . [vertical] integration'. Despite the valiant efforts of Chandler, Dunning, Williamson, Teece and others, the situation remains anarchic. From a policy perspective, the lack of convincing explanations of why firms integrate vertically has increased the temptation for economists to construct specialized, artificial models portraying vertical integration as having dubious social benefits. 'It has', as Coase (1972, p. 66) complained, 'encouraged men to become economic statesmen – men, that is, who provide answers even when there are no answers.' One is reminded of the scholar in Burton's *Arabian Nights* who, seeing no explanation for having testes, decided to 'divest' himself of his own with a razor. Hopefully the theory and evidence presented in the present study will contribute to the formation of a more balanced and realistic appraisal of vertical integration.

The second part of the study applies the entrepreneurial model of vertical integration and disintegration to several major issues in economic and business history, including foreign enclaves in less developed countries, large scale agriculture with dependent labor, and the putting-out system of manufacture.

Vertical integration is a complex phenomenon. It cannot be understood entirely in terms of the entrepreneurial motive, i.e. in terms of the efforts of innovators to overcome bottlenecks or information impactedness. Part III rounds out the study by discussing the most important competing and complementary explanations of vertical integration. In each instance an effort is made to examine the conditions under which the explanatory power of one theory is likely to be greater than the explanatory power of another theory. Here special attention is given to the implications of the Smith–Stigler (1951) thesis that the division of labor is limited by the extent of the market.

Finally, one appendix deals critically with Marx's theory of surplus value and neo-Marxist explanations of the employment relation (i.e. hierarchy), while a second appendix probes the relation between the shirking problem and firm size.

NOTES

1. See Baumol (1968, p. 65); Harris (1973, pp. 142–3); Kirzner (1973, pp. 14–16); Mueller (1976); Richardson (1960, pp. 104–6). Hébert and Link (1982) provide a useful survey of the meanings that have been given to the term entrepreneurship. See also chapter 19 of Casson's (1982) important study.
2. Bhatt (1976, p. 587) adds most perceptively that: 'For him [Marx], the whole process of economic change was an automatic process – and is this still not the view of modern planners? – resolving itself into the mere mechanics of amassing capital.'
3. On the importance of personal wealth, see Casson (1982, pp. 90–93).

4. Wilkins (1975, p. 219); C. Wilson (1975, p. 209).
5. To take one recent example, in international tourism the organization of group inclusive tours is largely controlled by firms of the affluent, tourist-generating nations (see McQueen 1983, p. 141). Vernon's hypothesis has received empirical support from a number of studies. See, for example, Adler (1970) and Dunning (1973, pp. 322–7).
6. See, for example, Thirsk (1978, pp. 8–9, 158–9).

PART I

Innovation, Information Impactedness and Vertical Integration

CHAPTER 2

Vertical Integration and the Employer–Employee Relationship

A firm is vertically integrated to the extent that it carries out the successive, technologically separable, productive operations or stages required to bring a product into existence and place it in the hands of the user. As the number of stages undertaken by a single firm rises, so does its degree of vertical integration. While the conceivable motives for vertical integration are many and, as we shall see later on, not always respectable, this study is primarily concerned with the entrepreneurial motive. On a more general level, it represents a contribution to the study of the organization of industry – that is, of the way in which the activities undertaken within the economic system are divided among firms, of the forces determining this division, and of how these forces have been changing over time (Coase 1972, p. 60).

The theory presented here is distantly related to Flaherty's (1981) which is concerned with how upstream actions can be directed with minimal effort when the downstream producer has imperfect information about upstream costs. But Flaherty's approach is ambiguous concerning predictions of efficient upstream direction by means of long-term contracts as opposed to vertical integration. Similarly, Arrow (1975) has argued that downstream firms seeking to make *ex ante* choices of technology have an incentive to integrate backward in cases where upstream producers have advance knowledge concerning the total supply of their product. However, it is difficult to visualize the kinds of information that would be available solely to intermediate goods producers. One does not, for example, have to be a farmer to know (or find out) that weather conditions were unfavorable at planting time. Indeed, in Japan, the general trading companies (*sogo shosha*) collect information on weather conditions and other factors influencing the price of cotton and convey this to Japanese spinners (ARTEP 1981, p. 181).

More generally, Etgar and Zusman (1982), building on previous research, have developed a model in which marketing intermediaries make use of the price mechanism to sell information about supply conditions to buyers and about demand conditions to sellers. The underlying condition for the emergence of such firms is their ability to sell information more cheaply than other sellers including, of course, their own customers. Second, there is the alternative to vertical integration of a futures market. As Arrow (p. 182) himself notes: 'Since the raw materials sellers do know their future product, they could offer valid contracts . . . in advance.' Given these alternatives, Arrow's hypothesis is not persuasive.

My theory is somewhat related to Blair and Kaserman's (1978) suggestion that divergent risk perceptions between firms at various stages of production provide an incentive for vertical integration.[1] But this takes uncertainty differences as given. It is fruitful to consider the source and direction of the divergence and to probe for methods of reduction and compensation. My position is closer to Buckley and Casson's (1976, p. 38) who state that: 'If the seller of an intermediate product is better informed than the buyer, but for one reason or another is unable to convince the buyer that the price requested is reasonable then the seller has an incentive to shoulder the buyer's risk either by taking over the buyer or setting up in competition with him.' It is still closer to Lall's (1978, p. 221) who suggests that vertical integration is related to the emergence of highly 'specific' products which embody new information (e.g. products produced with new technology).

The importance of *information differentials* in explaining vertical integration was first alluded to by Adelman (1955, p. 319) who suggested that in rapidly growing or changing industries 'a sluggish response will often force the growing [that is, the innovating] firm to provide its own supplies and/or marketing outlets.' Still earlier, Jewkes (1930) had noted a positive relationship between rapid growth and vertical integration. The possible linkage between vertical integration and economic change has also been explicitly recognized by Mighell and Jones (1963, p. 29). What follows can be regarded as an attempt to cast new theoretical and historical light on these little appreciated insights regarding new products and new markets.

Let us begin by considering the following scenario. An entrepreneur perceives that, as a result of changes in technology, tastes, incomes, or relative prices, good X, a new product, can be produced in a given region and sold, in the same or in a second region, for more than its cost of production. At this point it is important to underline Charles Wilson's (1957, p. 111) keen observation that 'it is misleading to consider the industrial revolution (as many textbooks do) merely in terms of undifferentiated commodities called cotton or woolens or iron. Such a treatment obscures the fundamental fact that the need to be met was for the highly specific version of such general categories of commodities and the relation between this fact and the consequent changes in industrial organization.' Good X should be understood in this sense of qualitative variation or 'mutation'. Newness of a product must also be understood in a relative as well as in the more obvious absolute sense. Wheat is a new product in a part of the world where it has not previously been grown; nuts and bolts are new products where they have not been manufactured.

To continue, the production of X will often involve one or more specialized and uncommon or novel (as opposed to routinely available) intermediate goods and services or 'operations' concerning which the entrepreneur has no special expertise. Suppose that the innovator seeking to minimize the cost of producing X offers to purchase these operations from appropriately talented independent local producers. In this connection it is well to recall that in its infancy even the industrial revolution produced surprisingly few basic skills not already familiar to mechanics.[2] The local producers, however, while possessing the necessary technical expertise, have not been producing such operations or, what comes to the same thing, have performed them only on a relatively small scale. The price offered by the entrepreneur is attractive, but how can the prospective operations' producers be sure that once they have made the necessary investments that the buyer will be able to fulfill his commitments to them? This problem has been raised by Richardson (1960, p. 83) who explains that the entrepreneur 'may have information sufficient to convince himself that this is the case, but others may not'. His request is, after all, rather eccentric. The local producers decline the innovator's offer; the risk is too great. For new products the problem of information incompleteness cannot be assumed away as in the standard textbook analysis.

This story, of course, illustrates Schumpeter's (1934, pp. 68, 86–7) insight about the reaction of the economic environment against one who wishes to do something new: 'Economic development consists primarily in employing existing resources in a different way.' But first entrepreneurs must gain control over these resources! Here we begin the second scene of our scenario. Does the entrepreneur seek to overcome this often tenacious, ignorance engendered resistance by *explaining* the nature of the economic opportunity to each unimaginative or inexperienced local producer in order to gain his cooperation? But this is no simple matter. The entrepreneur is faced with the significant problem of *information impactedness* which, as Williamson (1973, p. 318) explains, 'is partly an information asymmetry condition: one of the agents to a contract has deeper knowledge than does the other. . . . But more than asymmetry is implied. . . . It is also costly for the party with less information to achieve information parity.' Instead of bearing these information transmission costs, does the innovator offer a premium for uncertainty bearing – that is, does he raise his offer price in order to compensate the operations producers for their excessive (in their own eyes) uncertainty bearing?[3] Or, another strategy, does he seek to sooth their anxieties by writing detailed and inordinately costly contracts specifying in detail how the innovator will react in various conceivable contingencies?[4]

In addition to the direct cost of this course of action, it penalizes the innovator by reducing his ability to adapt to unexpected changes in market or technical conditions. In our example, the costs and hazards are intensified by his lack of technical know-how concerning the operation he desires to purchase. Alternatively, does the entrepreneur put up a forfeitable bond or place funds in escrow to mitigate the bankruptcy potential? Once again costs are imposed on the innovator and the vertical integration option becomes viable.[5] The possibility is at least raised that the entrepreneur will find that his *least costly* option for dealing with market bottlenecks is to purchase or rent the capital equipment and labor services of the local producers and employ them to produce the desired operations within his own firm.

The *employer–employee relationship* is, of course, a primal form of vertical integration. (It is important to remember, as will be illustrated more fully in chapter 7, that the *idea* of a new product for a new market is separable from its physical production; an entrepreneur may implement his idea either by hiring appropriately skilled laborers, i.e. forward vertical integration, or by purchasing the desired product from them, i.e. market exchange.) In the employer–employee relationship, what is purchased is not a specific outcome (or operation), that is, the results of the labor process, but an agreement on the part of the employee (the labor source) that in return for a specified contractual remuneration he will place his labor-power, or what Simon (1957, p. 184) calls his willingness to accept authority, at the disposal of the employer for a given period subject to a permitted range of uses. Of course, and this is usually forgotten, information transmission costs must be borne by the entrepreneur in the employer–employee relationship, as well as under the market exchange option. Therefore, it is not enough to speak of 'market failure' and to allege that resort to the 'firm' or 'internal organization' or 'authority' results in economies of information transmission. The basis of the presumed 'inherent structural advantage' must be explicated. The opening of this 'black box' remains to be accomplished.[6]

To be more specific with respect to information transmission, the employer sets up procedures or routines that the employee is told to follow. The key point is that this kind of communication – that is, communication regarding procedure – is less expensive than communication relating to a desired end result (substantive content). The successful performance of a 'terminal act' (here the acquisition of the desired operation) does not, as Arrow (1974, pp. 54–5) observes, 'require for assessment the entire probability distribution of states of the world but only some marginal distributions derived from it'. To put this in another way, the procedures and routines are 'sufficient statistics'; the information contained in the employer's orders to perform this or that task are a sufficient substitute for the knowledge of all the considerations that form their underlying rationale.[7] This is quite consistent with and, indeed, fleshes out Coase's (1952, p. 338) suggestion that 'the operation of a market costs something and by forming an organization and allowing some authority . . . to direct the resources, certain marketing costs are saved.'[8] In short, 'Do your job' is a parsimonious form of explanation.

On the other hand, the vertically integrating firm also has some inherent structural disadvantages. Owing to the entrepreneur's relative inexperience and lack of technical expertise, the integration option (the employer–employee relationship) will drive upward the production cost of the required operations. The less familiar the integrated operation is to the entrepreneur, the more his production cost will exceed that of an appropriately talented local producer. Often the entrepreneur will seize the opportunity to reduce this cost discrepancy by purchasing an existing experienced firm.[9] However, the purchase of an existing firm cannot eliminate the cost differential in favor of the local producers. This is the case because whether the entrepreneur integrates by means of internal growth, or by means of acquisition and merger, the installation of an unfamiliar technology provides his employees (or newly acquired partners) with the opportunity to shirk their assigned duties (see Silver and Auster in appendix 2). In addition, to the extent that vertical integration increases the absolute size of the firm, the shirking problem will be magnified. (The extent of the latter increase can, however, be reduced by divisionality and specialization.) The entrepreneur's costs rise if he tolerates this shirking or, alternatively, if he suppresses it by devoting additional resources (e.g. hired managers and foremen) to contract enforcement.[10] But over a range these extra production costs are smaller than the reduction in information transmission costs from vertical integration. The cost-minimizing extent of vertical integration is visualized more formally in chapter 5.

In my scenario the entrepreneur does not 'do it himself' in order to keep the profitability of good X a secret (Magee, 1981). Just the opposite is the case! The innovator would prefer to concentrate his managerial resources narrowly on X. His problem is that he cannot, at reasonable cost, convey his implausible 'secret' to those with the technical capabilities needed to produce the required operations at the lowest cost. Finding himself unable to secure the cooperation of the latter producers, the entrepreneur must direct his finite managerial resources into areas for which he does not have a comparative advantage. This in fact reduces the profitability of his innovation.

In the above considerations we can, I believe, find the origin of Knight's (1921, p. 271) 'enterprise system' in which a 'special social class, the businessmen, direct economic activity; they are in the strict sense the producers, while the great mass of the population merely furnish them with productive services, placing their persons and their property at the disposal of this class.' We can also appreciate Schumpeter's (1934, p. 89) conclusion that the 'capitalistic entrepreneur "leads" the means of production into new channels. But this he does, not by convincing people of the desirability of carrying out his plan . . . but by buying them or their services and using them as he sees fit.' Nevertheless, it is important to remember that vertical integration is neither an absolute requirement nor an iron-clad guarantee of entrepreneurial success. Our theoretical conclusions are much more modest: (1) vertical integration has the potential to facilitate the implementation of new ideas by reducing information transmission costs; (2) vertical integration should be understood in terms of more or less, rather than in terms of yes or no. The historical evidence presented below suggests that the cost-reducing potential of vertical integration is frequently realized in practice. Before turning to the case studies on the onset of vertical integration, however, some evidence regarding merger activity is considered. As Coase (1972, p. 73) has pointed out, 'the study of mergers should be extended so that it becomes an integral part of the main subject,' namely the structure or organization of industry. Chapter 3 represents a small step in this direction.

NOTES

1. See also Carlton (1979); Kihlstrom and Laffont (1979).
2. Coleman (1973, pp. 12–13); Gibbs (1950, p. 10). For example, the earliest eighteenth century textile inventions had mechanisms made of wood and could be operated by man or water power which remained the main power source well into the nineteenth century.
3. See Mueller (1976, p. 424). 'Uncertainty means that we do not have a complete description of the world which we fully believe to be true. Instead, we consider the world to be in one or another of a range of states. Each state of the world is a description which is complete for all relevant purposes. Our uncertainty consists in not knowing which state is the true one' (Arrow 1974, pp. 34–5). Within the framework of communications and statistical theory adopted in the present study, the term *information* is merely a negative measure of uncertainty (see Hirshleifer 1973, p. 31). Possibly one can distinguish between differences in information and differences in beliefs about probability of pay-off prospects. However, in the interest of tractability, I have assumed operational certainty on the part of the innovator and excluded differences in pay-off prospects from the analysis. These assumptions are decidedly neoclassical, but they serve to focus the analysis entirely on another area assumed away in neoclassical models, namely the issue of information transmission costs.
4. Arrow (1974, pp. 34–6); Goldberg (1980, 340–41); Teece (1980, p. 229). Williamson (1971, p. 115) points out that 'exhaustive stipulation, assuming that it is feasible, is itself costly. Thus although if production functions were known, appropriate responses to final demand or factor price changes might be deduced, the very costliness of specifying the functions and securing agreement discourages the effort.'
5. See Casson (1982, p. 14); Jensen and Meckling (1979); Richardson (1960, pp. 83–4, 117–18).
6. The analysis in this paragraph is based on a paper I circulated in June 1975 at a Conference on Individual Liberty and Governmental Policies in the 1970s and delivered in May 1976 at a Conference on the Economics of Information – see Silver (1981); see also Silver (1977, pp. 99–101).

7. Note, however, that even if economies of information exchange form the main rationale of the employer–employee relationship, as I am inclined to believe, other factors such as differences in attitudes toward risk and non-separability of the production function or 'team production' may also play meaningful roles – see Alchian and Demsetz (1972); appendix 2.
8. While it is quite true that widening the permitted range of uses of the employee's labor-power enhances the employer's ability to cope with uncertainty, it is misleading to suggest that employers desire authority because they face uncertainties. Due to economies of information exchange, employers would desire authority, that is the right to control the labor-power of others, even if they faced no uncertainties and could not alter the task assigned to an employee.
9. Hale and Hale (1962); Didrichsen (1972, pp. 212–16); Prescott and Visscher (1980).
10. On the most basic level the present study deals with the reason for the existence of firms (that is, of the employer–employee relationship). Another fundamental question, taken up in appendix 2, is why there is more than one firm producing any given product.

Hennart (1982, pp. 127–30) stresses the importance of managerial and organizational innovations and reductions in communications costs in mitigating the shirking problem and allowing larger equilibrium firm sizes. More specifically, he believes that the rising importance of direct foreign investment and the multinational firm since World War I and especially since World War II can be traced back to changes of the above kind which lowered internal organization costs relative to market transaction costs. This question of managerial and organizational innovations is dealt with in section 5.2.

CHAPTER 3

Mergers and Economic Change

Merger is a method for eliminating a valuation discrepancy in which a higher value is placed on the assets of a firm by nonowners than by owners. Thus it is reasonable to expect that fluctuations in the prevalence of such discrepancies will produce fluctuations in the merger rate. But, as Gort (1969, p. 627) contends, valuation discrepancies are more likely to exist in times and in industries experiencing rapid technological change or rapid growth in demand. Such 'economic disturbances', for example, 'alter randomly the ordering of expectations of individuals, with the result that some nonowners move to the right of current owners on the value scale.' Within the framework of my study, the individual who 'randomly' moves to the right can be equated with the entrepreneur.

Gort utilized Federal Trade Commission data on mergers in three-digit manufacturing industries for the period January 1951 through June 1959. The merger rate in an industry, that is, the ratio of the aggregate number of mergers in the industry over the entire period to the number of firms in 1954, was regressed on several measures of economic disturbance. The latter included an index of physical production to measure industry growth and, as proxies for technical change, the technical personnel ratio (the number of engineers, chemists, and surveyors per 10,000 employees), and the change in labor productivity from the beginning to the end of the period. As predicted by the economic disturbance and by the information reduction by retransmission hypotheses, the regression coefficients of these independent variables were consistently positive and approached or achieved statistical significance at conventional levels. Ralph L. Nelson (1959, p. 76) adds the important point that the intense merger movement at the turn of the century came after and during a period of accelerating industrial growth. High merger rates especially characterized the most rapidly growing industries (steel, meat packing, flour milling). Tilly (1982, p. 654) reports similar findings for Great Britain (textiles) and Germany (mining and metal production). Nelson (pp. 124–5) also found that in the US peaks in merger activity led peaks in industrial production and business cycles.

McGowan (1971) has presented some rough exploratory data on mergers in the United States, Great Britain, France, and Australia during the 1950s and early 1960s that also seem consistent with the hypothesis that more dynamic economies in which information impactedness problems would loom larger, experience higher acquisition rates. He suggests (p. 249) that 'low merger activity where it is not restrained by public policies may indicate that competition lacks the vigor which would compel rapid adjustment to changing conditions' – a very perceptive comment.

Nelson, Gort, and McGowan did not consider vertical mergers separately from other types of mergers.[1] Nevertheless, their finding of a positive relationship between rapid economic change and the overall merger rate is consistent with the information reduction by retransmission explanation of vertical integration. To go beyond this would require not only disaggregating the merger data, but taking into account such factors as technical change and, possibly, market growth.

The following chapter summarizes a mass of case study evidence on the onset of vertical integration. My point of departure is provided by Charles Wilson's (1957, pp. 105–6) suggestion that: 'Certainly a legitimate approach to modern economic history might be to trace the development from . . . the slow gathering of control over the different processes within a single industry to that outward seeking after control not merely of one industry but of ancillary industries and processes on which the so-called 'central' manufacture depends – in short to the vertical combine in which modern industrial development has reached (some might say, passed) its peak of self-fulfillment.'

NOTES

1. Between 1948 and 1976 some 1707 firms with assets of over US$10 million were acquired in US mining and manufacturing. Of these, 276 (or 16.2 per cent) represented horizontal combinations, while 179 (or 10.5 per cent) involved vertical integration and 1251 (or 73.3 per cent) were of a conglomerate nature (Spruill 1982, table 1.1, p. 4). During the period 1880–1911 a sample of 40 large German industrial enterprises acquired 56 firms of which 35 (or 62.5 per cent) represented horizontal combinations while 12 (or 21.4 per cent) involved backward or forward integration and 9 (or 16.0 per cent) involved diversification and integration (i.e. cases of takeovers of marketing enterprises or diversification into other sectors) (Tilly 1982, table 3, p. 638). Similarly, the largest 100 German manufacturing firms (as of 1907) acquired 158 other companies over the years 1887 to 1907, with 32 (or 20.2 per cent) involving vertical integration or diversification (as defined above) for the absorbing company (Tilly 1982, p. 639). Additional evidence on mergers is presented in Hughes and Singh (1980, table I–8, p. 19) and Goudie and Meeks (1982).

CHAPTER 4

The Onset of Vertical Integration

This chapter summarizes the main features of a large number of important case studies involving the introduction of new products for new markets. Aside from this entrepreneurial aspect, the sole criterion for the inclusion of a case was the availability of reliable, more or less explicit information pertaining to vertical integration. The studies are diverse in perspective and vary greatly with respect to time and place. Nevertheless, in each instance it is possible to detect a linkage between the innovation process and the subsequent onset of vertical integration.

4.1 CASE STUDIES FROM AMERICAN BUSINESS HISTORY

Automobiles

The creation and early development of General Motors provides a striking initial illustration. William C. Durant, a carriage maker, had a unique vision concerning the market for the 'horseless carriage'. In order to implement this vision, he found it expedient to go beyond the acquisition of existing assembly firms (horizontal diversification) to create a marketing–dealer organization and to purchase firms producing parts and accessories (Chandler 1962, pp. 118–20).[1] One General Motors acquisition in particular, that of Fisher Body in 1926, raises several important issues and therefore merits more detailed consideration. In the beginning, automobile bodies were individually constructed, open, and largely wooden. Then, in 1919, General Motors entered into a ten-year contractual arrangement with Fisher Body for the supply of metal, closed bodies. The production of the latter body-type, it should be noted, required investment in relatively specific stamping machines. An exclusive dealing clause that, in effect, required General Motors to purchase all its bodies from Fisher, served to protect the latter firm against opportunistic recontracting by General Motors (see further chapter 9). Similarly, several clauses provided General Motors with price protection.

The price was set on a cost plus 17.6 percent basis (where cost was defined exclusive of interest on invested capital). In addition, the contract included provisions that the price charged General Motors could not be greater than that charged other automobile manufacturers by Fisher for similar bodies nor greater than the average market price of similar bodies produced by companies other than Fisher and also included provisions for compulsory arbitration in the event of any disputes regarding price. (Klein, Crawford, and Alchian 1978, p. 309)

Fine.

But, as Klein, Crawford, and Alchian point out, in the next few years the demand for automobiles and closed metal bodies increased dramatically. During the twenty year period from 1900 to 1920, the total production of passenger cars increased by 1,901, 368 as compared to an increase of 2,549,618 from 1920 to 1929. From 1919 to 1926 the percentage of closed steel type bodies rose from 10 to 74 (Boyle 1974, p. 57). It would seem that the magnitude of these changes had been anticipated by General Motors but not by Fisher Body since, by 1924, severe disputes had broken out concerning such matters as price and whether the body plants should be relocated near the assembly plants. An uncertain Fisher Body dragged its feet or demanded compensation viewed as exorbitant by the more knowledgeable management of General Motors. In the end, General Motors decided that merger represented the efficient strategy for exploiting its insight into the potential of the automobile market. Similarly, prior to 1918, automobile tire fabric was produced by independent cotton mills. However, in 1919–20 rapidly increasing tire sales were associated with a pronounced shift from fabric to tire cord (Davis et al. 1938, pp. 91–3). Once again it would seem that the independent producers hesitated to make the necessary investments in specialized equipment, for the price of cord rose sharply and tire producers integrated backward into its production.

Oil

After the discovery of oil in western Pennsylvania in 1859, a single firm rarely performed more than two of the various operations involved in the oil industry, such as exploration, production, transportation to the refinery, refining, transport to the market, and marketing. All this began to change in the 1870s when a group of businessmen led by John D. Rockefeller, a refiner, founded Standard Oil (Ohio). The company gained control over Cleveland refineries, crude oil pipelines, storage facilities, and launched an export business from New York. (Prior to 1911, the chief product of the industry was kerosene, of which from one-third to one-half was exported.) Then, in the 1880s, Standard Oil added a nationwide marketing organization, tankers, pipelines, and even a few oil producing properties (A.M. Johnson 1976, pp. 192–3). By the 1890s Standard had become a major crude oil producer. The aggressive integration of the Standard Oil group into the marketing field is understandable in terms of the lagging introduction of new bulk handling techniques that significantly lowered distribution costs.

During the first few years of the oil industry's history, refined products were put up in barrels at the refineries and shipped by rail to jobbers who maintained warehouses and distributed to grocery stores and other dealers by horse and wagon. As soon as the tank car had become available, refined products were shipped in bulk to local 'barrelling and marketing' plants where they were put up in barrels, cans, and other containers for distribution to dealers and farm customers. These bulk plants, however, which called for storage tanks, a cooperage plant, and a barrel warehouse, were more expensive than earlier warehouses, and the small jobbers may have been slow in constructing the new facilities. The later adoption of the tank wagon to make deliveries to local retailers in populous areas, which likewise required additional investment, may also have proceeded more slowly than the Rockefeller interests thought desirable. (McLean and Haigh 1954, p. 67)

But during the pre-1911 period Standard Oil was far from alone in its vertical integration drive. The explanation offered by de Chazeau and Kahn (1959, pp. 84–5) is quite consistent with information impactedness considerations. The Guffey Petroleum Company (the direct predecessor of Gulf) realized that it needed to build pipelines and a refinery to create a market for its Spindle-top Texas crude oil. Significantly: 'Neither at the outset nor when the Mellons joined the venture did the presence of Standard seem to have dictated the recourse to integration. Instead ... *vertical integration was apparently essential in the early stages of the industry's development to create an industry where none had existed before: "Guffey had Texas oil but Texas had no oil industry"*' (italics added).

Later on, the major refiners offered inducements for independent gasoline retailers to sell their products. The latter were not sufficiently attractive, for refiner-owner service stations proliferated in the 1920s and 1930s. In evaluating this development it is well to note de Chazeau and Kahn's (1959, p. 298) observation that the creation of chains of refiner-owned gas stations was a major innovation: 'Although nothing seems more obvious today than that special retail outlets should have been provided to satisfy the soaring demands of the automobile for gasoline, lubricants, and service, this view is strongly tinged with hindsight; it unfairly minimizes the break that drive-in service stations made with the past.'

The efficient aspects of vertical integration in the oil industry find additional confirmation in the events following the Supreme Courts's May 1911 dissolution of the Standard Oil Trust (founded in 1882). During the next two decades the parent company (Jersey Standard) and the principal severed companies became vertically integrated in their own right. Standard Oil (Indiana), for example, a refining and marketing company, integrated backward into transportation and crude oil production. Moreover, independents such as Shell and Phillips entered the industry and also found it necessary to integrate vertically. As A.M. Johnson (1976, pp. 191, 197, 199–202, 213–14) notes, the hydra-like post-dissolution record of the companies suggests that vertical integration was a source of lowered costs rather than a mere anti-competitive ploy. Vertical integration helped to solve the monumental information impaction problems generated by rapid growth and innovation in the oil industry.

The Growth of the Nation: Machines for Farmers, Steel for Cities

Due to westward expansion the acreage and production of wheat almost doubled from the end of the Civil War to 1880 and the expansion continued into the 1880s. Given the sharp increase in demand for harvesting machinery, it is not surprising that Deering Harvester Company in the 1890s built a rolling mill, purchased a blast furnace, and acquired iron-ore, coal, and timber property (Phillips 1956, pp. 11, 15). In the late 1880s Andrew Carnegie, then a large producer of steel rails, saw that the future lay in urban housing and backed his vision by purchasing and converting the Homestead Steel Mill and Duquesne Steel Works from rail-making to the fabrication of structural steel shapes. Louis M. Hacker (1968, pp. 351–2) well describes the conditions of those times:

> The era of the modernization of America's cities had begun: tall buildings were being erected of stone and masonry (Why not with steel skeletons?); new bridges were being built to speed urban rapid transit; elevated structures on which ran steam trains were being erected in cities; streets were constantly being torn up to lay great pipes for water and sewage disposal; the transmission of electricity for lighting and power, the beginning of the urban electrical trolley – all required new and different kinds of steel for fabrication and generation. . . . Carnegie was in the van; it was no wonder that the profits of the company increased so sensationally in the 1890s – though almost one-half of the decade was in depression.

Under the leadership of Henry C. Frick, the Carnegie Company became a vertically integrated enterprise with its own iron-ore mines, ore ships, and railroads. Much later, in 1911, a witness before the Stanley Committee explained that Carnegie's 'genius was to realize that the real time to extend your operations was when nobody else was doing it' (quoted in Hacker 1968, p. 358).

Insurance

The history of the life insurance industry also illustrates the importance of the information impaction problem. During the late nineteenth century the latter industry experienced spectacular growth; from 1885 to 1910 per capita holdings rose more than fourfold from US$40.69 to US$179.14. Also, as predicted by our theory, in this period the marketing system was drastically altered. The general agency system was replaced by the branch office system – that is, independent soliciting firms were replaced by salaried solicitors (Keller 1963, pp. 9, 67–9). A quite similar pattern manifested itself in the property and casualty insurance industry during the booming period since the Second World War. Increasingly, the system of independent agencies (dealers) was supplanted by direct writing in which insurance companies sold insurance through their own salesmen or through the mail. This trend toward vertical integration was especially significant in the rapidly growing area of automobile insurance (Etgar 1978, p. 252; Joskow 1973, pp. 379, 389).

Meat Packing

Swift saw the profitability of shipping refrigerated meat from Chicago to eastern cities and established branch offices and retail outlets there. This was necessary because doubt-filled jobbers feared that the meat would spoil before they could sell it, but refused to invest in refrigerated warehouses (Porter and Livesay 1971, pp. 109–10). In addition, Swift had to combat the belief that the shipped meat was poisonous! (Krooss and Gilbert 1972, p. 151). Beyond this, when the Grand Trunk Railroad, 'unwilling to assume the risk itself . . . insisted that Swift or some other agent furnish the cars . . . Swift marshalled the necessary capital and ordered ten. . . . When [Andrew J.] Chase's car removed the objections to its predecessors, Swift entered the production of refrigerator cars' (Aduddell and Cain 1973, p. 94). Somewhat earlier, in the 1870s, large prominent integrated firms which slaughtered, packed, and marketed meat became prominent in the midwest. This, as noted by Walsh (1982, pp. 133–6), can be traced to the sharp increase in the size of the market for midwestern meat due to the application of the technology of ice packing. During the summer, ice which had been cut and stored during the winter in specially constructed icehouses was used to pack meat. The integrated firms bore the rather significant costs of erecting their own icehouses. The traditional channels of animal supply, however, remained quite adequate and, consequently, the large packing companies did not integrate backward into animal raising (Porter and Livesay 1971, p. 172).

Backward Integration into Primary Production

During the 1940s and 1950s, the demand for fruit and vegetable varieties adapted to canning and freezing increased sharply. In this instance the traditional sources of supply were not adequate, so a growing number of processors integrated backward into growing and made the necessary investments in specialized harvesting machinery. This trend, as might be expected, seems to have been especially strong in Wisconsin, a state whose farmers were usually specialists in dairy farming (Mueller and Collins, 1957).

Vertical integration was also noteworthy in the dynamic poultry industry. This is not at all surprising since, as Mighell and Jones (1963, p. 68) observed: 'In the main, the commercial broiler represents a new product produced in new areas.' The years following 1950 saw a true revolution in which broiler chickens were raised indoors in individual cages with automated food delivery. Some feed firms supplied fuel, broiler houses, equipment, and litter to their grower customers on credit (Seagraves and Bishop 1958, p. 1821). But besides this 'contract farming', a significant fraction of production was carried out by the hired employees of feed millers, or processors willing to make the required specialized investments in houses, feeders, and the like. The latter firms included some that owned hatching egg layers, hatcheries, growing houses, veterinary services, research labs, and more (Roy 1963, pp. 36–7). From 1955 to 1977 vertically integrated broiler production rose from 2 per cent to 10 per cent of total output (Brooks 1980, p. 202). During the same period, for closely related reasons, the percentage of egg production accounted for by firms combining market egg production with other stages in the egg subsector rose from 1.5 to 37 (Schrader 1980, p. 222). The very sharp growth beginning in the 1950s of commercial feeding in the Southern Plains (Texas, Kansas, Oklahoma, Colorado, and New Mexico) has been accompanied by the emergence of large commercial feedlots that have integrated backward and forward into such operations as cattle raising, restaurants, grain elevators, and feed manufacture (J.R. Martin 1979, pp. 106–9; note the discussion of earlier 'bonanza farms' in section 8.4).

The Question of Forward Integration into Retailing

George Eastman (Kodak) perceived that amateur photographers constituted a large market for a paper-based firm using a (perishable) gelatin emulsion to replace the glass plates utilized by professionals. In order to minimize costs, Kodak integrated backward into direct production of paper, celluloid, and lenses and forward into the manufacture of a standardized camera and the establishment of wholesale and retail outlets (Chandler 1977, pp. 297–8). A cigarette manufacturer, James B. Duke, who was the first to recognize the growing market for that, then, new and exotic product, set up purchasing operations in tobacco-growing areas (Chandler 1962, p. 27). Quaker Oats, the breakfast cereal that took the nation by storm, was created in 1882 by the oatmeal producer, Henry P. Crowell. Crowell, like Duke, purchased directly from farmers (Chandler 1977, pp. 293–4). Significantly, in the food and tobacco cases, where unlike the cases of refrigerated meat, autos and cameras, the innovators could rely on long-established retail networks, forward integration into retailing was minimal (Livesay and Porter 1969, p. 498). One exception to this statement seems actually to be consistent with the underlying principle: in the nineteenth century, American Tobacco's *foreign* subsidiaries and affiliates did enter retailing (Wilkins 1975, p. 219).

4.2 CASE STUDIES FROM OTHER PARTS OF THE WORLD

The Effects of Economic Warfare

Beginning with the decree of February 22, 1806 in which Napoleon banned imports of English yarns and textiles into his empire, economic warfare radically altered the prospects and orientation of Ghent's textile industry. Most importantly, the Spanish market was closed, while access was gained to the French and, to some extent, the continental market. As Dhondt (1969, p. 44) notes, the years from 1806 to 1810 'were painful as well as exacting years: manufacturers lacked experience, undoubtedly capital was in short supply and new machinery failed to function'. During this period of ferment the emergence of new products and markets was accompanied by a significant vertical integration trend. 'The originality of the new firms lay not only in their immense size, but also in their unique organization. There was a definite trend towards the creation of vertical concerns ... Factories comprising spinning, weaving, and printing works were frequent in the cotton sector of the industry. In the wool and flax spheres of production, the same manufacturers concentrated on both spinning and weaving. They also undertook the dressing and bleaching. Furthermore, Ghent manufacturers ... themselves attended to the sale of their goods' (Dhondt 1969, pp. 46–7). At least one firm, L. Bauwens, produced its own machines.

Bessemer's Testimony

Henry Bessemer (1813–98), who created the process of producing iron or steel capable of being run into a mold or ingot in a fluid condition, provides in his autobiography a nearly perfect illustration of the causal relationship between information impaction and vertical integration.

And yet, with all this newly developed power, I was paralyzed for the moment in the face of the stolid incredulity of all practical iron and steel manufacturers. . . . None of the large steel manufacturers at Sheffield would adopt my process, even under the very favorable conditions which I offered as regards licences, viz., 2 pounds per ton. Each one required an absolute monopoly of my invention if he touched it at all. This I fully made up my mind to resist, by adopting the only means open to me – namely, the establishment of a steel works of my own in the midst of the great steel industry of Sheffield. My purpose was not to work my process as a monopoly, but simply to force the trade to adopt it by underselling them in their own market, which the extremely low cost would enable me to do. . . .

Thus were established the first Bessemer Steel Works. (quoted in Edwards and Townsend 1961, pp. 11–12)

The existing producers hesitated to invest in Bessemer plant, so the inventor had to do it himself. Note the unimportance of secrecy considerations.

Chemicals

Beginning in the 1870s, new vistas for the dye stuffs industry were opened by significant progress in organic chemistry that made possible the use of previously neglected materials such as napthalene and anthracene and the production of hundreds of new dyes. German firms such as Badische responded by abandoning their earlier practice of selling dyestuffs through import firms and wholesalers and began to deal directly with the dyehouses. This was followed by sales-service systems and the establishment of experimental dyehouses (Haber 1958, pp. 169, 174–5). Then, in the first quarter of the twentieth century, the opening up of new fields of chemistry facilitated an enormous broadening of product range. Haber (1958, p. 169) argues that 'it was this rapid diversification which compelled businesses to extend their operations and to integrate their production.'[2] Chandler (undated, pp. 18–19) adds that special facilities were required for storage, distribution, and transportation because the finished chemicals were often toxic or otherwise dangerous. Of even greater importance, marketing called for a sales force of trained chemical engineers to explain the use of their products to industrial customers, especially the new synthetics. Once again it appears that independent firms up and downstream from the chemical producers were unwilling to undertake these specialized investments in facilities and staff.

Automobiles

During the four years from 1921 to 1925, production of the English automobile manufacturer Morris Motors, the first to assemble a relatively light, low-cost car, exploded from 3,000 to 55,000 per annum. Maxcy (1958, pp. 367–70) notes that acquisitions of suppliers 'were more or less forced on [Morris] by the need to obtain sufficient supplies of certain components to match his rapidly expanding output of cars'. For example, when Morris offered Hotchkiss a contract to take 500 or 600 engines a week, the latter company refused, saying the best it could do was about 300. Morris purchased the plant and within six months had production up to 500 engines. Morris, later Lord Nuffield, was described by two of his old business associates in the following terms: 'Morris always had second sight. He liked to think of himself as an engineer, but really he was a prince of commerce, because he had an instinct to know what people wanted, to know what the next man was thinking' (quoted in Edwards and Townsend 1961, pp. 36–7). More recently, riding the wave of demand for small, economical cars, the sales of Nissan Motor Company (Datsun) in the US rose from just under 19,000 in 1965 to over 150,000 five years later. Finding itself faced with significant bottleneck problems, Nissan, beginning in 1965, ceased to charter conventional freighters and began to operate a fleet of specially designed ships for the transport of motor vehicles. Then, in 1967, Nissan completed the construction of Hommoku Wharf in Yokohama with its 38 acres of storage and shipping facilities to handle its exports. Finally, in 1969, the firm built a large dock and warehouse complex in California (Rae 1982, pp. 1, 83, 95–6).

Forward Integration into Wholesaling

Beginning in the middle of the 1950s, rising personal incomes together with other factors vastly increased the potential market of the Japanese home electric appliance industry. But the manufacturers were confronted by the difficult problem of finding distribution channels for new products such as television sets, washing machines, refrigerators, and vacuum cleaners. The most successful approach was innovated by the Matsushita Electric Industrial Company. In areas outside Tokyo where independent wholesaling facilities were underdeveloped, Matsushita purchased an ownership interest in existing small wholesalers and consolidated them into regional 'National Product Sales Companies'. In the Toshiba and Hitachi model the manufacturers established sales branches which wrote agency contracts with independent wholesalers (Tamura 1971, pp. 283–5).

4.3 CASE STUDIES OF EARLY INDUSTRIALIZATION IN BACKWARD AREAS

Gerschenkron (1962, p. 353) has pointed out that rapid industrialization 'started in several ... countries from very different levels of economic backwardness' and added that 'these differences in points – or planes – of departure were of crucial significance for the nature of subsequent development.' One economic development variation of special interest for the present study is Gerschenkron's Proposition 2: 'The more backward a country's economy, the more pronounced was the stress in its industrialization on bigness of both plant and enterprise' (p. 353; see also Richardson 1960, pp. 85–6). This result is understandable within the framework of the present research. Since information impaction problems increase with the degree of economic backwardness, our theory predicts a prominent role for large, vertically integrated firms.[3]

England and Germany Compared

Kocka (1978, pp. 550–2, 578) notes that the trend toward vertical integration was both earlier and stronger in Germany's industrial revolution than in England's. By way of explanation he points to the relative backwardness of German industry.

It is not easy to explain this difference adequately, and more research needs to be done. ... Probably the trend was connected with the relative backwardness of German industry. ... Industry in Germany has less continuity with the pre-industrial structures than in England. In the industries most important for German development (engineering and the extractive industries), the early industrialists frequently had no established, developed trading structure to utilize. In addition, the producers therefore took over the marketing, when it was a matter of selling technically complicated products.... Frequently, early factory-owners seem also to have had a deep mistrust of the independent distributor.... To bring together as many functions as possible, from the provision of the raw materials to final sales was thus both an expansive and a defensive wish.... Vertical integration appeared early above all in the mining industry.... This was apparently true for the early pioneering entrepreneurs, who founded their firms on 'green field' sites.

The firms in the German electrical industry produced everything from telegraphs to power stations (Kocka 1971, p. 561). Problems of the same kind as those confronting the early German industrialists also led to the formation of 'development blocks' in Sweden during the early 1900s. A clear example is provided by the newly born electrical engineering industry whose firms found it necessary to apply their insight to the electrification of the nation. Even as late as 1929, electrical engineering firms contracted for the extension of the telephone network (Dahmén 1970, pp. 65, 385).

Family-Oriented Industrial Combines

The same kinds of advantages of establishing development blocks in relatively backward areas to mitigate information impactedness problems may also lie behind the otherwise puzzling emergence in Japan of huge, family controlled *zaibatsu* combines. (The focus here is on the size and diversity of these enterprises, the family orientation serves to mitigate the shirking problem; see further, section 5.2.) The latter, which consisted of the 'big four' (Mitsui, Mitsubishi, Sumitômo and Yasuda) plus six others, controlled, until their dissolution in 1945, financial, commercial, and manufacturing companies in different industries (Lockwood 1954, p. 227).

The opening of ports to foreign commerce after 220 years of seclusion in 1859 at the end of the Tokugawa period and the Meiji Restoration in 1868 threw open the doors to the economic modernization of Japan. One entrepreneur who grasped this new opportunity was Iwasaki Yataro (1834–85) who, with government help, founded a shipping firm (the Mitsubishi Company) in 1873. In 1878 Iwasaki moved into maritime insurance. Two years later he added warehousing, foreign exchange, and discount banking to accommodate merchants who used his shipping services. Finally, he built a modern shipyard (Hirschmeier and Yui 1975, pp. 38–41). The existing Japanese merchants, however, were quite unprepared to service the export–import needs generated by the opening of a modern economy. Hence in 1891 and 1892, the Japanese Spinners' Association found it necessary to begin their own cotton import companies. Again, in order to market its coal, Mitsui opened offices in various Asian cities. From this experience–investment base the Mitsui *zaibatsu* went on to import the main needs of the *zaibatsu* and the cotton spinning industry, including machinery, raw cotton and oil, and to export yarn, cloth and raw silk. Later, with the growth of heavy industry and the emergence of a chemical industry, the other *zaibatsu* also founded their own trading organizations (Hirschmeier and Yui, p. 185).

As Hirschmeier and Yui point out, the unique role of the *zaibatsu* not only in trade but in strategic guidance of industrial development must be traced to the pioneering conditions of the Japanese economy. For the same reason, the task of establishing an appropriate system of financial institutions also fell to the *zaibatsu* and other industrial enterprises. 'They established their own banks to serve their own enterprises. Beginning with the *zaibatsu* which one after the other founded their own *zaibatsu* banks, to the smaller entrepreneurs, this tendency became obvious; these banks were called instrumental banks for being instruments of the industrial ventures' (Hirschmeier and Yui 1975, p. 185).

A closely related pattern of family oriented industrial organization is found today in many less developed countries (Leff, 1978). The 'managing agency system' of the East Indian Archipelago and India strongly features vertical integration.[4] In India this system was declining prior to 1970 and was legally abolished in that year.

The Story of an Entrepreneur

Several previous themes are drawn together in the career of Francesco Matarazzo who, in 1881, emigrated from Calabria, where he had been in the hog and lard business, to Brazil where he founded the largest industrial complex in South America. Matarazzo's central insight, as he later recalled, was that: 'Fats that came from the United States . . . were very expensive to buy, while in Brazil the pigs were swarming' (quoted in Dean 1969, p. 61). Matarazzo moved from dealing in hogs to rendering lard. However, instead of packing lard in the re-used wooden kegs of American imports as other local manufacturers were doing, Matarazzo achieved great success by putting his lard into cans. Not long afterwards, he bought a cannery, a lithography shop for making labels, a saw mill to supply his box plant, and even foundaries and machine shops to repair his equipment. Matarazzo also sold his product directly to retailers.

Meanwhile, Matarazzo began to import wheat flour from the United States and Argentina as well as rice from Cochin China. In 1899 he opened a wheat flour mill and went on in 1904 to make the cotton sacking for the flour himself. Matarazzo purchased several coastal freighters and shipped in them the various raw materials he needed for his lard and flour milling enterprises. Finally, since the existing dock facilities of the Docas de Santos Company were backlogged and plagued by pilferage and breakage, Matarazzo built separate docks for his vessels. Dean (1969, pp. 61–3) notes that other industrialists also exhibited a tendency to self-sufficiency and his explanation reflects the importance of the information impaction problem. 'Matarazzo and the other industrialists, operating in a frontier economy were anxious above all to reduce the uncertainties of raw material supply and of transport and power.'

4.4 CASE STUDIES ON THE ROLES OF MERCHANTS AND LANDOWNERS

The information acquired by merchants and large landowners during the course of their business and other activities goes far to explain their often repeated pioneering roles in production. As Charles Wilson (1957, p. 107) nicely puts it, uniting the roles of merchant and manufacturer mitigates 'the friction between the former who alone knew what the customer would buy, and the latter, who was often more interested in persuading the merchant to take what he had always made'. Similar considerations underlie the unification of land-owner and land-user.

Textiles

In the sixteenth century the merchant–manufacturing system was concentrated in those industries in England, the Low Countries, and Italy that were heavily engaged in exporting (Jeannin 1972, pp. 4, 77). The Fuggers, for example, not only owned mines, ironworks, and foundries, but also manufactured fustian (a mixed cotton) on their estates in the Ulm region. This pattern was especially characteristic of the West European textile industry. Specifically, merchants took over production and employed the previously independent craftsmen as wage laborers (Lis and Soly 1979, pp. 68–9). Thus in southwestern Flanders (Hondschoote), export merchants took over the production of the so-called 'new draperies' which, in fact, were serges made of worsted yarn spun from long-staple wool. In the newly formed Lyonese silk industry, the export merchants integrated backward beyond production to the direct import of raw silk. The tendency toward vertical integration was especially strong among merchants who, driven by religious persecution from established textile centers such as Aachen, settled in rural areas where experienced masters were rarely to be found (Barkhausen 1974, pp. 228–9). Much earlier, in the thirteenth century, independent craftsmen dominated the locally-oriented Parisian district, while the booming internationally-oriented cloth trade of Flanders and Artois was directed by great 'drapers' or 'cloth merchants' who were better placed than the local artisan to be aware of the demands of distant consumers (Halphen 1964, pp. 190–91; Landes 1966, p. 11). In the Artois area merchants such as Jean Boine Broke produced wool and grew the plants from which dyes were made on their own lands, and also employed masters in the manufacture of cloth (Van Werveke 1954, p. 253).

In late eighteenth century Norwich and Yorkshire, the strong continental demand for worsted led cloth merchants to enter manufacturing. In 1792–3 Benjamin Gott, a woollen cloth merchant who aimed at the United States market for fine cloth, realized his dream by importing high quality wool and building England's first really large woollen mill (Heaton 1931, pp. 45–52). With the aid of Samuel Slater, a mechanic who brought pirated textile technology from England, the well-to-do American merchant Moses Brown founded Boston Associates in the late eighteenth century. The latter firm moved from the production of cotton yarn into textiles and made its own machinery (Krooss and Gilbert 1972, p. 92; Ware 1931, pp. 25, 31–2, 49–53). Francis C. Lowell, a Boston merchant, had the business acumen to forsee the profitability of the application of power loom technology to the US cotton industry. In 1813 he established at Waltham Massachusetts the Boston Manufacturing Company, whose 'secret formula' for success is outlined by Ware (1931, pp. 60–61) as follows: 'The old mills had their yarn woven into stripes and plaids which required more or less skill in weaving and which varied in fineness and fashion. The Waltham company started producing plain, coarse, white sheeting made from number fourteen yarn which the power loom could turn out easily and which could be used for almost all purposes, especially by the western pioneers.' of course, the firm was quite successful in spite of the postwar slump and the increased imports of high quality British cloth.

Prior to the advent of synthetic dyes, India exported to the English textile industry a dyeing material made from the indigo plant. With the application of power to the manufacture of cotton, the demand increased sharply in volume and became more exacting in terms of quality. Buchanan (1934, pp. 35–6, 53) summarizes the organizational shifts that took place in response as follows: 'From independent merchants buying finished indigo (from peasant producers), the indigo dealers . . . became, by a gradual process of evolution covering nearly a century, owners of land and independent producers with every stage of the process under their own control.' (But on this process see also chapter 10.) Also during the first half of the nineteenth century India offered significant opportunities in the cotton textile area for entrepreneurs with connections in the world economy. As Brimmer (1955, pp. 560–66) points out, the Parsis who had long traded in cotton and thereby developed strong connections with British merchants integrated into the manufacture of cotton textiles. Similarly, in late nineteenth century Brazil, especially in textiles, the earliest manufacturers were importers who had, of course, become familiar not only with specialized domestic needs but with foreign modes of production and finance (Jeffreys 1954, pp. 68–9). Later, in the 1950s, the overwhelming majority of entrepreneurs who participated in the rapid industrial development of Pakistan belonged to trading families. Industrial entrepreneurs began to be drawn from other groups in the middle and later 1950s when, as Papanek (1967, pp. 40, 45–6) observes, 'the rewards had become widely known.'

Shipbuilding
Beginning as early as 1603 the United East India Company found 'the requirements of the trade so specific that they chose to produce their own East Indiamen' (Unger 1978, pp. 9, 14). For the Orient trade the merchants required a large cargo vessel capable of doubling as an effective warship. The solution was found in a unique hull design. It would seem that the shipwrights were unwilling to lay out relatively large sums over a couple of years to construct a suitable shipyard, so the Company gave up its original policy of ordering its vessels from independent builders and began instead to hire its own ship carpenters. A similar system prevailed at Venice for large merchantmen from about 1425 to 1570 (Lane 1934, p. 115).

Iron and Steel
The Baltimore Company, which pioneered the expansion of the American iron industry, was founded in 1731 by merchants with connections in London (the principal outlet) and the outports as well as in the West Indies and the mainland colonies (K. Johnson 1966, pp. 72–6). Between 1830 and 1860 the United States railroad network exploded from 30 miles to 34,000 miles. In the 1840s a handful of merchants, who recognized the scope of the market for rails offered by the coming of the railroad, built blast furnaces and substituted steam for (inadequate) water power to drive the rolling mill

machinery. Indeed, the first president of Bethlehem Iron, Alfred Hunt, was a merchant (Porter and Livesay 1971, pp. 57–9, 79). In nineteenth century Germany, traders played key roles in the production and working of iron and steel. Franz Haniel, a coal trader, took over a lower-Rhine smelting works and then moved into extraction, shipbuilding, and the manufacture of railway equipment. Friedrich Krupp, the pioneer of cast steel and founder of the Krupp concern, also began as a trader (Kocka 1978, p. 519). Indeed, Kocka points out that despite 'anti-capitalist currents in German public opinion' which portray the leading entrepreneurs as craftsmen or technically qualified individuals, 'the information available indicates the extremely strong and perhaps even dominant role of merchants and traders in the German industrial revolution.'

The Role of Retailers

Charles Wilson (1975, p. 194) comments that the British firm Lever Brothers, founded in 1885, was the 'perfect exemplification of the eighteenth century maxim that "the tradesmen always stands at the head of the manufacturer" '. Lever, recognizing the potential mass market for a quality, free-lathering soap in affluent England, transformed himself from a grocer into an industrialist. In 1895 the firm, by that time the largest soap producer in the UK, began manufacturing operations in the US. In the latter country the development of a market for silks and fine fabrics for women's fashions led to a sharp increase in the production of Lever's Lux Flakes, from 100,000 cases in 1915 to over one million by 1918. Similarly, the introduction of washing machines foretold a large demand for Rinso, the first granulated laundry soap (1919). Predictably, the years 1918–19 saw Lever Brothers adopt a new selling policy in the US: jobbers were replaced with a nationwide, exclusively Lever sales force.

Also in the later nineteenth and early twentieth centuries in Britain, multiple shop retailers emerged and went into the direction of manufacturing in trades such as milk, outerwear, bread, flour, wallpaper, and paint. The most famous of these shop-owners was, of course, Thomas Lipton who, taking into account the enormous capacity of the prosperous British market, began trading in tea in 1889 and soon thereafter purchased tea plantations. Further, after an extensive search in Denmark, Sweden, and Russia for additional supplies of ham and bacon, he also founded a hog-packing plant in Chicago (Buckley and Roberts 1982, pp. 87–9; Mathias 1967, pp. 179, 187–9, 195, 252, 258).

Landlords and Agricultural Innovation

Germany in the eighteenth century experienced rapid change in agricultural practices, including cultivation of the fallow by means of turnips, clover, peas, beans, lentils, hemp, and potatoes. This was apparently triggered by a greater demand for animal fodder for stall-feeding, which in turn was partially a response to the increased demand for manure. In several areas noble landowners and bourgeois lessees founded estate villages that utilized wage labor and replaced the villages of the independent peasantry (Mayhew 1973, p. 42). Later, in the nineteenth century, the isolated natural economy of northern Russia began to crack under the impact of land and water steam transportation. The ensuing dramatic changes in the agricultural geography of the country had been preceded, as Pavlovsky (1968, p. 70) informs us, by a trend during the course of the century in which the Russian gentry established agricultural associations and studied and imitated foreign improvements. Agricultural innovation also played a major role in the great Japanese economic take-off in the middle of the nineteenth century. And, as in the Russian case, the so-called 'cultivating landlords' typically played the main role. As Waswo (1977, p. 33) explains: 'Most landlords of the Meiji era were well educated. . . . They were better able than other farmers to understand the world outside the village and to negotiate with outsiders,' as well as to take advantage of 'new railways and other improvements in transportation which facilitated the commercial sale of crops'.

Landlords in Industry

In Britain in the middle of the sixteenth century the new process of smelting iron by means of blast furnaces, as opposed to bloomeries, was first introduced on a large scale by prominent Sussex landowners. The latter, understanding the potential of the London market, exploited their own timber and ore and integrated forward into smelting and casting (Crossley 1974, pp. 24–5). Later, beginning in the middle of the seventeenth century, landowners with deposits of coal and iron and stands of timber played a noteworthy role in fostering industry. Much earlier, during the rapid urbanization of Rome after the foundation of the Empire in the first and second centuries CE (Common Era) estate-owners invested in large kilns to produce the needed bricks (Bloch, 1941). Jumping forward in time from ancient Europe to Pakistan in the 1950s, we find that a significant number of industrialists were Yusufazai Pathans who had previously been wealthy landlords. The connection made by Papanek (1967, p. 50) is that: 'Living on the main trade route to Afghanistan, they were involved in trade and transport before they became industrialists. Their large cash crops also linked them to the market. Just as cloth merchants became textile-mill owners, Yusufzai sugar cane growers became sugar-mill owners.'

NOTES

1. An earlier pioneer, Albert H. Pope, finding merchants to be hesitant to purchase his novel Columbia Gasoline Tricycle, initiated his own package delivery service (Rae 1959, chapter 9).
2. In 1887 the 100 largest German manufacturing and mining firms (in terms of share capital) included twelve from the chemical industry, of which two were confined to production and did not integrate forward into sales or backward into raw materials. By 1907 the representation of chemical firms had risen to seventeen, with only two confined to production. The source of these data is Kocka (1980, tables 3.4 and 3.5).
3. The preference in less developed countries for vertical integration may also reflect an attempt to replicate the organization of successful firms in the developed countries. See also section 5.8.
4. On the managing agency system, see: Allen and Donnithorne (1954b, pp. 52–3); Bain (1966, pp. 12–14); Brimmer (1955, pp. 560–61); Kidron (1965, pp. 22–3).

CHAPTER 5

A Model of Vertical Integration and Disintegration with Supporting Evidence

5.1 THE COST-MINIMIZING EXTENT OF VERTICAL INTEGRATION

The next step is to formalize the entrepreneurial theory of vertical integration put forward in chapter 2 and supported by merger and case study evidence in chapters 3 and 4. In figure 1 the upstream and downstream operations or stages required to bring the new good X into existence and place it in the hands of the user are arrayed in order of increasing dissimilarity to the production of X itself. That is, as we move to the right the operations encountered by the entrepreneur have less and less in common with X production in terms of scientific, engineering, production, and marketing knowledge and experience.[1] This arrangement is responsible for the positive slope of the *MIPC* curve which shows the marginal increase in production cost from integrating an operation over the production cost of an appropriately talented independent producer.[2] To use a term that has begun to win a secure place in the literature, movement to the right increases the diseconomies of scope.[3]

The horizontal *MRITC* curve, on the other hand, reflects the simplifying assumption that the marginal reduction in information transmission costs that results from integrating an operation instead of purchasing it from an independent firm is invariant with respect to the particular operation integrated.[4] The latter quantity, it should be recalled, is the savings from hiring inputs and managing them instead of

A Model of Integration & Disintegration

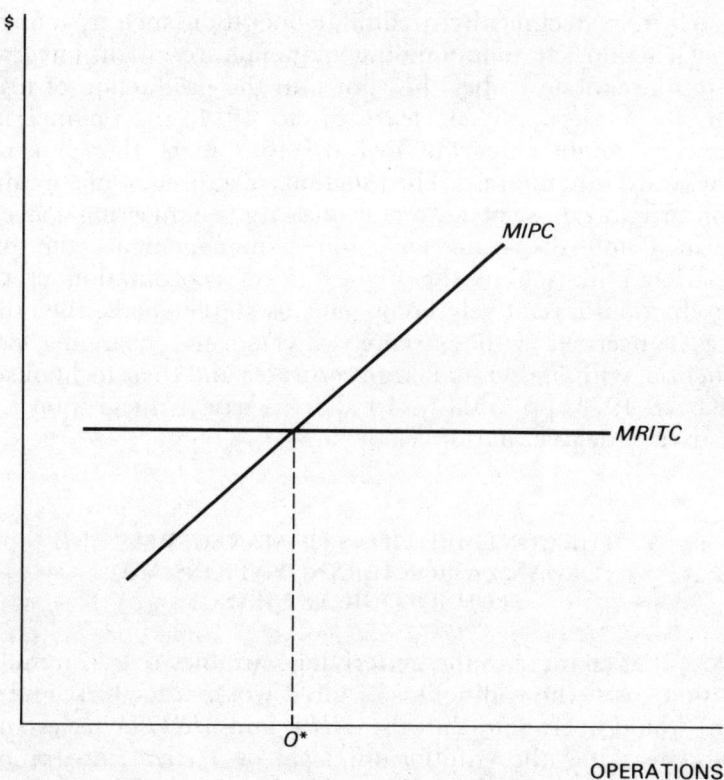

(Up and downstream operations arrayed in order of decreasing technical similarity to good X)

Figure 1: *Cost-Minimizing Extent of Vertical Integration*

communicating the need for a novel operation to independent producers. To simplify the exposition it is assumed that a fixed amount of the entrepreneur's total potential managerial effort is deployed in the production of X itself (and perhaps in other products as well).[5] The residual managerial effort is available for integrating operations and for communicating with independent producers. The cost-minimizing extent of vertical integration for the innovating firm is O where *MIPC* is equal to *MRITC*.

To make this more concrete, an oil refining company, for example, might integrate into crude production but not into a much more technically dissimilar operation such as refinery construction. Or an automobile manufacturer might integrate into automobile bodies, but not into the production of tires. Or as in Germany, at least up to 1914, the engineering concern might integrate forward into marketing but not backward into mining: 'The functions of a director of a mining concern and those of a director of a large engineering concern seemed too disparate for unified management: the one restricted himself to the highest level coordination of the production of relatively homogeneous staple goods; the other was concerned with extremely diverse and changing production, with, individual large contracts and their technology' (Kocka 1978, pp. 561–2). In short, vertical integration is a matter of degree, not of yes or no.

5.2 THE CONTRIBUTIONS OF MANAGERIAL AND ORGANIZATIONAL INNOVATIONS AND TECHNOLOGICAL CHANGE

Note that changes in the underlying variables (e.g. communication costs, the willingness of hired workers to shirk, and so on) would operate to shift the $MIPC$ and $MRITC$ curves and, thereby, alter the equilibrium level of vertical integration. Indeed such changes might well take on an economy-wide secular character. For example, one organizational innovation whose importance for efficiency has been stressed by both Chandler (1962) and Williamson (1975, chapter 8) is the shift beginning in the early 1920s by several large American corporations, including DuPont and General Motors, from functional organization to multidivisional internal structure. It is posited that this change from centralized to decentralized management favors behavior patterns more like those predicted by the classical profit-maximization (cost-minimization) model. Of course, it is not difficult to think of counterarguments. Armour and Teece (1978) have provided some empirical evidence for the petroleum industry that seems to support the so-called M-form hypothesis. One truly ancient technique for mitigating the shirking problem is to select managerial personnel from the ranks of relatives and close personal friends. This technique has obvious defects, but its potential is reflected in the huge Japanese *zaibatsu* combines of pre-Second World War Japan (see section 4.4). More recently, the paternalistic practices of some Japanese firms, including the granting of virtual lifetime employment to employees, has attracted favorable attention in the United States.

More generally, if Hennart (1982, pp. 127–30) is correct in stressing the importance of nineteenth and twentieth century managerial innovations mitigating the shirking problem, the results (*ceteris paribus*) would be not only larger firms but more vertically integrated firms due to a rightward shift of the *MRITC* curve. But technological considerations would also have to be taken into consideration in predicting secular trends. If, as Rosenberg (1963, pp. 422–6) seems to imply, nineteenth century industrialization tended to cause 'technological divergence' between X production and the various upstream and downstream operations, the result (*ceteris paribus*) would be reduced vertical integration due to a leftward shift of the *MRITC* curve.[6] The introduction of modern computer networks would probably operate in the opposite direction by providing more effective controls over shirkers. It goes without saying that these issues deserve theoretical clarification and far more empirical attention than they have received up to now.

5.3 VERTICAL INTEGRATION AND THE PASSAGE OF TIME

An additional implication of the analysis is that (*ceteris paribus*) vertical integration to exploit newly perceived economic opportunities will be, on the average, a short-run phenomenon.[7] Thus the model takes into account not only mergers but 'dismergers' or the breaking up of firms. With the passage of time, the merits of good X (and of its innovators) will be demonstrated. This, of course, will also diminish the uncertainties of independent operations producers. The latter, at least initially, may very well arise from among the personal contacts of the innovator: employees, relatives, and friends. In short, as time passes the information transmission costs of using the market to obtain the desired operations will decline. Consequently, the marginal reduction in information transmission cost (*MRITC*) will approach zero for all operations. This trend is indicated in figure 2 by the downward shift of the *MRITC* curve from time 1 to time 2.

Of course, increasing experience on the part of the innovator with the integrated operations will also drive down the marginal increase in production cost (*MIPC*). Experience facilitates routinization: employees can be told to look up the appropriate rule and penalized if they fail to do so.[8] Routinization relieves the pressure on the time the innovator can devote to preventing shirking by his employees including management personnel. Dudley's (1972) regressions illustrate this point. They show that learning from production experience by the firm (measured both in terms of cumulative output and elapsed time) played a relatively important role in increasing productivity in the metal products sector of Columbia from 1959 to 1966. Dudley concludes that learning by workers and firms was more important than the effects of increased capital per worker or larger scale, but *'learning by firms (in the sense of the development of a system for controlling production and nonproduction activities) may be as important as learning by workers'* (pp. 666, 669; italics added). The experience consideration is reflected in figure 2 by the downward shift of the *MIPC* curve from time 1 to time 2 *for those operations previously integrated in time 1*. Thus, *ceteris paribus*, the cost-minimizing extent of vertical integration for an innovating firm can decrease or remain constant but cannot increase over time. On the average, then, the cost-minimizing extent of vertical integration will decline with the passage of time.

5.4 VERTICAL INTEGRATION AND 'QUIET TIMES'

Having boldly stated the implication of decreasing or constant vertical integration over time, it is necessary to retreat somewhat and qualify the analysis. With the passage of time the entrepreneur might reduce the amount of his managerial effort deployed in producing good X itself (see section 5.1).

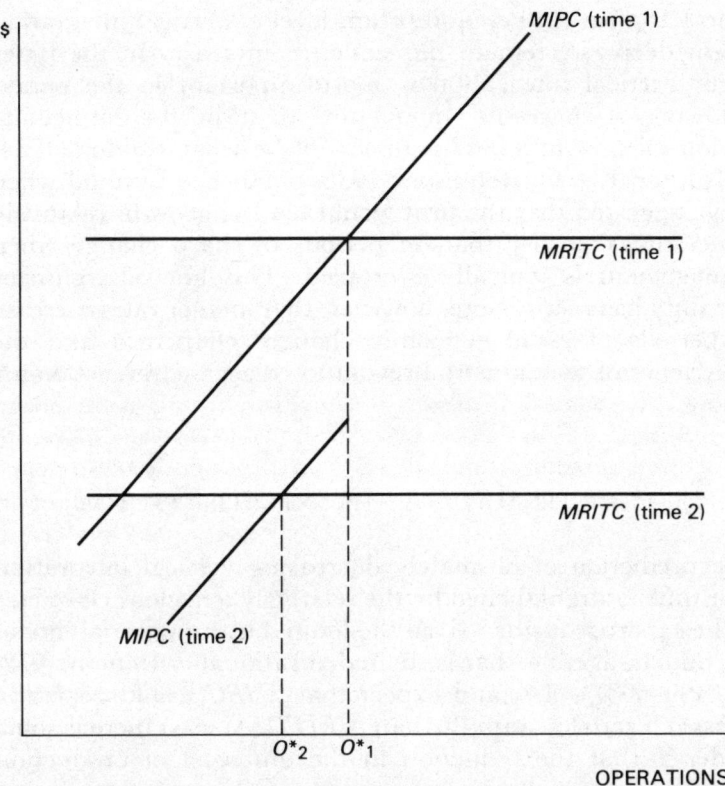

(Up and downstream operations arrayed in order of decreasing technical similarity to good X)

Figure 2: *Changes Over Time in the Cost-Minimizing Extent of Vertical Integration*

Increased experience in X production might make this possible and desirable. Alternatively, a reduction in entrepreneurial effort on the X front might result from the entry of new producers and a consequent reduction in the price of X and the entrepreneur's equilibrium output of X. The diversion of the freed managerial time to operations upstream and downstream from X would mitigate the shirking problem in time 2 and, for this reason, would operate to shift the *MIPC* curve to the right *for all operations*. Depending on the magnitude of the downward shift of the *MRITC* curve from time 1 to time 2, the equilibrium level of vertical integration might decrease, remain the same, or increase. In the latter event vertical integration is more important in the period following a successful innovation than in the immediate period of innovation. This may well be what Kaldor (1934, p. 75) and E.A.G. Robinson (1935, p. 50) had in mind when they suggested that the firm would tend to grow in relatively 'quiet times' rather than in periods of sharp change when management is typically overtaxed. This line of argument certainly has merit. Note, however, that merger rates increase in periods of rapid economic change (chapter 3) and the experience of the industrial revolution discussed in section 5.8 below.

5.5 THE TENACITY OF THE EXPERTISE FACTOR

The prediction of ultimately decreasing vertical integration over time is strengthened by the relatively tenacious character of the expertise factor. Given the limited learning capability of the human agent – that is, bounded rationality (Simon 1972, pp. 499–503) – I would expect that $MIPC$ would generally approach zero less rapidly than $MRITC$. At least there is some evidence that the reduction in the unit cost of production resulting from a given increase in cumulative production, a measure of experience, decreases with the experience level (cumulative production). Apparently the typical experience curve can be approximated by:

$$Y = an^{-b}$$

where,

Y = unit cost
n = cumulative production in units
a and b = parameters of the model.

Certainly, the exponential form fits the case of Ford and its Model T (Intercollegiate Case Clearinghouse 1975; Boston Consulting Group 1972, pp. 12–13). Cohen (1975, pp. 88–9, 120–32) prefers an S-shaped curve in which learning reaches a maximum level as cumulative output increases.

$$Y = e^{a-(b/n)}$$

where,

> Y = output in units per worker
> n = cumulative production in units
> $a, b > 0$
> e = base of the natural logarithms.

As cumulative output becomes very large, output per worker approximates to e^a. The logistic curve, Cohen reports, gives the best general fit for a sample of firms in South Korea, Singapore, and Taiwan.

All in all there is good reason to expect that with the passage of time entrepreneurs will ultimately peel-off the least familiar operations to appropriately talented independent firms including sub-contractors and franchisees.

5.6 ORIGINAL INNOVATORS COMPARED WITH NEW ENTRANTS

Another implication of the analysis is that, *ceteris paribus*, the predicted decline in vertical integration over time will be more pronounced for the X industry as a whole than for the original innovator(s). New firms entering the X industry in time 2 will share the lower *MRITC* of this time but, since they have not actually experienced the necessary upstream and downstream operations, they will not share the lower *MIPC* of time 2.[9] There is no learning without doing.

5.7 AN ECONOMETRIC CHALLENGE

It goes without saying that the perspective on vertical integration developed here creates difficulties and dangers for empirical and policy analysis. This is illustrated by a sophisticated study by Levin (1981, p. 216) who suggested that if vertical integration promotes efficiency, then those firms in an industry that are more fully integrated should earn higher profits than less integrated firms. Such a test might be helpful in the initial stages of the exploitation of a newly perceived economic opportunity if, and this is questionable to say the least, there was sufficient variation in the degree of vertical integration across firms producing X. But new products are typically introduced by one firm or by a mere handful of firms. As is well known, peak profitability for a new product occurs in the growth stage before many new firms have entered the industry and eroded away the extra profits of the innovator (Parker 1974, pp. 16–17). Thus Levin's test is inappropriate in the later stages of the life cycle of a new product when it is most easily applied. We have already seen that as a result of learning by doing the original innovator(s) in an industry, say the oil industry, will on average be more integrated than later entrants. I see no reason, however, to believe that older oil refining firms will earn higher profits. Levin's failure to observe that vertical integration (crude production plus refining) increased oil company profits in 1948–57 or 1958–72 in no way demonstrates that vertical integration failed to promote efficiency and raise profits from the 1880s into the 1920s or 1930s.[10] There is good reason to believe it did (see chapter 4). Neither does it mean that there would be no social losses if the older refiners were required to divest themselves of crude production. In fact, this would squander the production experience painfully acquired by these firms.

Let us now consider some case studies involving vertical disintegration.

5.8 CASE STUDY EVIDENCE

The Changing Roles of Agriculturalists

As noted in section 4.4, English landowners played an important role in fostering industry in the initial stages of the industrial revolution but, as Jones (1967, p. 26) points out, as the eighteenth century progressed English landowners leased off their mines and ironworks and withdrew more and more from active participation in non-agricultural ventures.[11] Another instructive example is provided by the experience of central Germany with sugar beet cultivation from the 1850s onward (Perkins 1981, pp. 86–104; Tipton 1976). The invention of the steam kettle and a well developed railway network combined to open up new markets for beet sugar. This potential was exploited by the owners of sugar factories who often cultivated the beet themselves. The expansion of sugar beet growing was accompanied by a significant trend toward the emergence of large holdings worked by wage labor. Obviously, the sugar industrialists knew far less about farming than the 'peasants' they hired, but the latter were apparently unwilling to make the necessary investments in artificial fertilizers, special stubble-ploughs and steam-ploughing, powerful draft animals, and additional labor for hoeing, thinning, and hilling.

However, toward the end of the nineteenth century the picture began to change in directions predicted by our theory. The trend toward land concentration was arrested and small peasants increasingly grew sugar beet for the market. At this time 'a reduction in the optimum size of holdings' was noted. One writer observed in 1907:

Although it is difficult to compare the profitability of different farms, it appears to be the case that with intensive cultivation it lies precisely with those holdings whose size permits the operator to control the teams and workers. (quoted in Perkins 1981, p. 99)

Of course, what had increased was not the shirking problem which was evident to all in the 1850s, but rather the familiarity of ordinary farmers with the market for sugar beet. Therefore, Perkins' (1981, p. 98) observation that 'the later nineteenth century witnessed a decline in vertical integration in the industry, whereby sugar-milling companies divested themselves of their large landholdings and increasingly relied upon the purchase of beet from growers' is not in the least surprising.

The Changing Roles of Merchants and Retailers

Manchester's cotton goods merchants had become merchant–manufacturers in the eighteenth century when they innovated machine-spinning. But in the early nineteenth century they once again became 'pure merchants . . . conducting the home trade from their warehouses and the export trade through the Exchange' (Farnie 1979, p. 61). During Sweden's early industrialization, the first engineering enterprises, lumber and pulp mills, and furniture factories were typically run by merchants who had either traveled abroad and made contacts with foreign businessmen or were familiar with the nation's urban scene. By the 1890s, however, technically trained individuals had begun to replace merchants. Still later in the interwar period independent sub-contracting firms took over the production of intermediate operations from the firm marketing the final product (Dahmén 1970, pp. 62–3, 73, 271–2). It was noted in section 4.1 that in the early days of refrigerated railway cars in the later nineteenth century, meatpackers integrated forward into branch houses in Eastern cities while the meatpacker Swift even integrated into retailing. The latter operation was, however, surrendered in short order as shipped meat gained in public acceptance. Later a similar evolution was felt in meat wholesaling: 'Over the period 1929–58 the number of packer-owned branch houses fell by 50 percent (from 1157 to 522) while the number of independent merchant wholesalers increased by almost 100 percent (from 2,225 to 4,482)' (Aduddell and Cain 1981, p. 365).

Under the pressure of the rapidly growing demand for gasoline, many oil companies had found it expedient to construct and operate their own gasoline stations. However, due to a combination of continued building and a slackening of the growth of the market after 1926, the supply of service stations caught up with the demand. Predictably, the 1930s witnessed a very significant disintegration movement in which most integrated oil companies abandoned direct operation and leased their stations to independent operators. The latter, frequently, were the by now experienced service station managers. Under the new circumstances prevailing in 1936, the Standard Oil Company (Indiana) recognized that 'by placing our stations in the hands of independent dealers and by giving them the flexibility and private initiative of the independent operators, the sales trend should be reversed and our profits increased' (quoted in McLean and Haigh 1954, p. 291). Actually, at this time several companies withdrew entirely from marketing. The sale of gasoline to independent refiners grew in importance.

This trend is confirmed by both Census of Business data and a questionnaire circulated to the leading integrated refiners. The latter revealed that from 1936 to 1953 'in both gasoline and heating oils, more companies increased than decreased their percentage of total sales through such distributors' (de Chazeau and Kahn 1959, pp. 535–6). After the middle of the 1930s when the use of fuel oils for home heating greatly increased, many oil companies had begun 'to carry their distillates through their bulk plants, to engage in burner sales and burner maintenance activities, and in some instances to participate in truck deliveries to the homes of consumers' (McLean and Haigh 1954, p. 513). But, as the above data suggest, with the passage of time the major refiners began to place heavy and increasing reliance for the performance of such operations on independent wholesalers and distributors.

The Industrial Revolution and its Aftermath Compared

During Britain's industrial revolution beginning about 1780, entrepreneurs such as Wedgwood (ceramic ware) and Boulton (steam engines) built up vertically integrated concerns that participated not only in manufacturing and marketing, but also, characteristically, in importing supplies, factory building, transport, banking, mining, and estate development. But Chapman (1979, p. 216) explains that after about 1810 'as the ancillary transport, financial, and marketing services reasserted the economies of specialization . . . the empires built by the Industrial Revolution pioneers were dismantled'. Habakkuk (1968, pp. 4, 7) points out that, unlike the industrial revolution of the eighteenth century, during England's 'classic age of traditional capitalism' in the nineteenth century *'when the adaptations required were gradual'* (italics added):

The successive stages of production and the various processes were often separate from each other. . . . In much of the steel industry, for example, smelting, steel-making, and rolling were separate. And in the shipbuilding industry there was a division of labor between the marine-engineering, the producers of various components and the builders of ships . . . This division was much less evident in the complex of activities that went under the name of the engineering industry but here too, in certain major sectors of the industry there was a division of function between the consulting engineer responsible for design and the manufacturer responsible for production.

Note the contrast of these observations with the 'quiet times' hypothesis outlined in section 5.4.[12]

Machinery Production in the Textile Industry

The earliest American textile manufacturers such as Boston Associates produced their own machinery (Ware 1931, pp. 25, 31–2, 49–50, 63). However, from 1845 to 1865 the last textile firms gave up producing textile machinery. By this time not only were machine-building skills more widely dispersed, but the pace of technical innovation had slowed. The large number of patents granted for modifications and attachments to existing machines suggests that the independent textile machinery makers were willing to make the modest refinements and modest investments requested by their textile mill customers until the turn of the century (Navin 1951, pp. 17–22; Strassman 1959, pp. 78, 88–90, 102). Thus it would appear that the sources of this noteworthy episode of vertical disintegration can be traced to the kinds of factors identified in our theory. Similarly, in Germany during the 1850s and 1860s most of the textile manufacturers who had earlier built their own machines released this task to independent firms (Kocka 1978, pp. 551–2, 562). Another useful illustration is provided by the even more youthful Brazilian cotton textile industry which in and after the 1850s was dominated by integrated mills combining all operations from spinning to finishing. However, unlike the early American and German textile manufacturers, the Brazilian industry which developed later did not design and produce its own equipment. Instead, Brazilian 'mill entrepreneurs first decided on the type of cotton cloth salable in their local markets. With this coarse cloth in hand they approached the local machinery importing houses . . . or went directly to overseas machine shops' (Stein

1957, pp. 34–5, 39–40). The explanation is that the international development of the textile industry had greatly reduced the information transmission costs to Brazilian innovators of purchasing machinery, while the extra costs of integrating machine production were magnified by the industrial backwardness of the Brazilian economy.

Fabrication by Copper Firms

Herfindahl (1959, pp. 207, 211, 239–40) calculated that between the pre- and post-First World War period the real price of copper (i.e. the nominal price deflated by a final products price index) declined by 46 per cent. This huge drop in price was due to a major innovation in the mining and processing of copper ore which made it possible to shift from selective to non-selective practices, that is, to the mining of low-grade ores in large quantities. The post-First World War period was at the same time one in which the 'Big Three' copper mining firms (Anaconda, Kennecott, and Phelps Dodge) integrated forward into fabricating which previously had been in the hands of independent firms (McCarthy 1964, p. 68). Here the opportunity was provided by the needs of construction (strong, flexible, non-corrosive alloys in the form of sheets, strips, and rods; flexible metal hoses; large- and small-diameter seamless tubing) and, somewhat later, from the rapidly growing electrical and electronics industries (magnetic and non-magnetic wires; cables and coils of both large size and miniature dimensions) (Moran 1974, p. 38). But as familiarity with the new copper markets made possible by the changed cost structure increased, independent fabricators began to proliferate so that the Big Three's share of fabricating capacity declined from a high of close to 70 per cent prior to the Second World War to 50 per cent in 1955. The firms that entered mining in the 1950s were not integrated into fabricating. Moreover, of the Big Three only Phelps Dodge absorbed the greater part of its own mine output in its own fabricating plants. Kennecott sold the greater part of its output to independent firms while Anaconda did not own enough copper to service all its fabricating needs (McCarthy 1964, pp. 71–3, 85, 93).

Disintegration in Ultramodern Industries

Even the computer industry is not immune to vertical disintegration. In 1964, IBM introduced its third generation of computer systems. This system/360 line was designed around a hybrid circuit called Solid Logic Technology (SLT). At first all SLTs were produced by IBM's own components division. But with the increased commercial availability of integrated circuits, IBM in 1966–7 decided to phase out the manufacture of all discretes and purchase these devices from outside suppliers (Harman 1971, p. 21; D.D Martin 1977, pp. 298–9). Similarly, the values of the Vertical Industry Connections Index (VIC), a novel measure of vertical integration developed by Maddigan (1981)[13] for the pioneering Xerox Corporation, show that its degree of vertical integration rose substantially from 1963 to 1967 and declined precipitously from 1967 to 1972.

Some Leading Firms Compared

While Eastman Kodak began marketing cameras in the late nineteenth century, the Polaroid Corporation's first full year of sales was 1949. Quite consistently with our theory the latter firm was much less vertically integrated than the former: Polaroid sub-contracted camera manufacture to other firms and purchased its negative material from Kodak under long-term contracts. (Apparently the problem of opportunistic recontracting did not loom large in its calculations, see chapter 9.) Then, in the early 1970s, Polaroid introduced the SX-70 system which it realized had truly revolutionary market potential.

There was no need to time the development of the picture. Other features included automatic ejection of the picture from the camera by a small electric motor (powered by a fresh battery present in each film pack), single lens reflex viewing and focusing, a folding design that allowed the camera to be carried conveniently in a large pocket or purse and less need for periodic cleaning of critical mechanical components inside the camera. (Intercollegiate Case Clearinghouse, 1976, p. 4, 7)

Apparently sub-contractors did not make an adequate response, for Polaroid moved sharply in the direction of vertical integration. It designed and built a color manufacturing plant and a camera assembly plant. Then, in response to the short shelf life of the batteries it purchased, Polaroid began to produce its own.

The United States automobile industry really began its commercial existence in 1900 and experienced its first meaningful growth only in 1907. Ford was incorporated in 1903, General Motors was formed in 1908, and Walter P. Chrysler, a General Motors graduate, became president of Maxwell–Chalmers in 1923 and took full control in 1925. Interestingly, Chrysler is the least vertically integrated of the 'Big Three' (see Boyle 1974, p. 16). It is also worth noting that while the later maturing British automobile industry certainly had its share of vertical integration (see the discussion of Morris Motors in section 4.2), it was nevertheless true, as Hannah (1980, p. 59) points out, that British manufacturers did not operate steel-pressing or electrical-components plants. Also, Monteverde and Teece (1982a, p. 212) note that the leading firms of the still later Japanese automobile industry are less vertically integrated than the American. If this is the case, the question is whether this can be attributed to differences between the Japanese and American business cultures, or to increased familiarity with automobiles and their markets with the passage of time.

Repeated Patterns of Integration and Disintegration

In a world of change information impactedness problems may become insignificant at one point in time only to re-appear strongly at another leading to a new surge of vertical integration. For example, in the early days of the American industry, pig iron producers generally mined their own ore, but after about 1830 they and their successors, the producers of crude steel, increasingly purchased their ore from independent mining companies. When, in the later 1890s, the Carnegie Company and other leading firms began to mine ore this reversed a 65-year trend to less backward integration by

American pig iron and crude steel producers (Mancke 1972, p. 221). The pattern of repeated episodes of vertical integration and disintegration is especially marked in the textile industry. The improvement of the power-loom in the early 1820s facilitated the mechanization of weaving and encouraged the expansion of coarse spinning. In about 1827 firms that combined spinning and weaving began to appear in Lancashire.

By 1841 they employed more workers than the separate spinning and weaving firms in every cotton town except Rochdale. Thereafter they increased in importance and embodied by 1850 31 percent of the firms but 52.5 percent of the spindles, 60.8 percent of the labor force, and 82.6 percent of the power-looms employed in the English cotton industry and an even higher proportion of those employed in Lancashire. (Farnie 1979, pp. 313–14, 318)

But Farnie adds the significant fact that, starting in the 1850s, the trend toward the vertical integration of weaving and spinning was reversed. The power-loom was technically perfected and its implications for spinning and weaving were more widely comprehended, which revived the tradition of vertically disintegrated enterprises. The decade of the 1880s completed the dethronement of combined firms. Earlier in the 1790s the improvement of the Crompton mule, together with the increased availability of better quality cotton, had substantially reduced the cost of producing good quality yarns. Spinners, however, hesitated to make the required investments in the relatively expensive cast-iron mules and high quality cotton. Weaving firms, better aware, perhaps, than spinners of the potential market for high quality cotton cloth became impatient and integrated backward into spinning (Edwards 1967, pp. 8–10, 126, 131–3, 200–1). Of course, with the passage of time weavers found it increasingly easy to obtain the desired yarn qualities on the market from independent spinning firms and yarn merchants.

Around and after 1900 the American textile industry, unlike the British, adopted large new machines such as the Northrop bobbin-changing loom which required simultaneous changes in spinning and weaving. In the United States spinning and weaving were integrated, while in the British industry they were mainly performed by independent firms (Markham 1950, p. 76; Strassman 1959, pp. 92–3). Lazonick (1981a, p. 32) reports:

From the mid-nineteenth century until after World War II, the degree of vertical specialization in Lancashire was increasing. In 1930 only 26 of the more than 2,000 cotton yarn and cloth producers in Britain had their own marketing facilities, and only 19 of these combined spinning and weaving. These firms had their origins in the nineteenth century, many in the early phases of the industrial revolution when some form of integration of production and distribution was a requirement of doing business.

Lazonick's point that the oldest firms were more likely to be vertically integrated than the newer entrants is consistent with the argument presented in section 5.6.

In the 1950s and 1960s with the growth of the 'fashion industry' and the development of new products, producers of artificial fibers and chemical firms (for example, Courtaulds and ICI in Britain, Celanese Corporation in the United States, Snia Viscosa in Italy, and Rhône–Poulenc in France) integrated forward into such operations as textile production, garment-making and wholesaling, and backward into wood pulp (Coleman 1973, pp. 17–19). This trend will also be reversed.

5.9 MARXIST PERSPECTIVES ON VERTICAL INTEGRATION

But Lazonick (1981a, pp. 33–4), a neo-Marxist, appears to confuse cause and effect when he places the blame for the alleged technological inertia of the British cotton industry on vertical disintegration. Elsewhere, Lazonick (1981b, pp. 106–7) has accused vertical disintegration of mysterious defects including absence of 'coordinated decision making' and 'excessive competition' and asserted that: 'The British cotton textile industry was unable to make the transition from nineteenth-century competitive capitalism to twentieth century corporate capitalism.' He adds, gratuitously, that 'neoclassical economics seems to have much the same problem.'

The problem is Lazonick's. Within the framework of the theory presented in this study, vertical disintegration is simply an equilibrium adjustment to the absence of pronounced economic change, not its cause. As Habakkuk (1968, p. 11) has stated, in the 1890s and early 1900s the merger boom was much more powerful in the US than in the UK. Here it should be recalled that the merger rate can be viewed as an index of economic dynamism (see chapter 3). The cotton industry of the United Kingdom had become routinized and consequently it also became relatively vertically disintegrated. If British entrepreneurship failed the explanation must be sought elsewhere.

Permit me to add at this point that Marxist theory seems to be subject to cycles of its own with respect to vertical integration and disintegration. During the 1930s, Marxist Soviet economic administrators also adopted a mechanical approach to the question, but they erred in exactly the opposite direction. Comparing the youthful industry they had inherited from pre-revolutionary days with that of the United States and Western Europe, they concluded that vertical integration was a source of technological backwardness! Granick (1967, p. 151) reports that 'during the years of the first Five Year Plan, virtually all the participants in reported discussions accepted in principle both specialization by process and the creation of specialized component plants.' (As we shall see in chapter 10, the actual practice was quite different from the theory of the planners; Soviet firms came more and more to adopt an extreme degree of vertical integration that came to be called 'universalism'.) Along the same line, Giannola (1982), an advocate of publicly subsidized development investment in Italy's Mezzogiorno, compares favorably the firms in the center and the north which have changed 'from the production of a product to the production of a few components' (pp. 73–4) with the 'still mainly vertically integrated' southern firms that arose in the latter half of the 1970s in several rapidly growing industries. He fears (p. 89) that: 'Further development of the Mezzogiorno along the present lines would clearly reveal in the long run a continuance, rather, than the disappearance, of dependence together with a revival of the traditional factors giving rise to dualism.' Policy proposals without either theory or history are a dangerous medicine.

5.10 THE ALLEGED MODERNITY OF VERTICAL INTEGRATION

It is worth emphasizing that vertical integration is 'modern' only in the limited sense that it accompanies rapid economic change. While Chandler's (1977, p. 1) dictum that 'modern business enterprise took the place of market mechanisms in coordinating the activities of the economy and allocating its resources' is generally true, so also, if we are patient, is the opposite position. After a longer or shorter period of adjustment the 'visible hand' tends to recede into the shadows if not into invisibility. The confusion on this issue is reflected in the popular and, sometimes, even in the scholarly literature, when successful Japanese automobile firms are held up as an example of 'vertical integration', by which is meant that they rely heavily on independent contractors!

An exception is, of course, provided by the continuously innovating firm or industry which would tend to manifest a continuously integrated structure. A prime example of this is Kodak which integrated into the raw-materials stage of film production. But even Kodak no longer operates retail stores in major cities (Chandler 1977, pp. 298, 374). In the automobile industry most of the products of the assembly and components divisions are highly interrelated, which means that a change at one point may cause a chain reaction of changes.[14] Monteverde and Teece (1982a) aggregated, perhaps somewhat arbitrarily, automobile components into six sub-systems 'based on expert evaluation of the degree of technical interrelatedness among the components' (p. 210). With the exception of the 'Electrical' sub-system, the coefficients of the five dummy variables taken alone do not exhibit a significant relationship with backward integration. Nevertheless, the set of five systems-effect dummies, taken together, seems to contribute to the explanatory power of the model. Moreover, Monteverde and Teece also found that General Motors and Ford have a positive and statistically significant 'preference for backward vertical integration when the components are firm-specific and their design must be highly coordinated with other parts of the automobile system' (p. 212). At the same time the industry has been subjected to major changes in market demand and government regulations, technical innovation, and, since 1923, annual style changes. Therefore, from the information impactedness standpoint, it is not surprising and not reprehensible that the 'Big Three', General Motors, Ford and Chrysler,

> are extensively integrated into the production of all aspects of the industry. This integration includes the production of all types of electrical and mechanical components, the production of pistons, rings and engines (including the operation of the forging facilities necessary for their production), the stamping of frames and other portions of the cover as well as a variety of related activities. (Boyle 1974, p. 17)

It should be noted, however, that with the passage of time retailers became more willing to make the necessary investments in working capital and, consequently, that automobile manufacturers abandoned branch retail outlets in favor of independently owned, franchised dealerships.

The petroleum industry, which has a relatively vertically integrated structure, is also ranked among the most innovative United States industries (Teece 1976, p. 174). Since 1900, refining has been characterized by a series of major changes in products (e.g. high-octane gasoline) and new technical processes (e.g. thermal and catalytic cracking) mainly under the influence of increased demand for improved quality and quantity of motor gasoline. One small piece of econometric evidence is consistent with our emphasis on the importance of the gains from information reduction by retransmission in a continuously innovative environment. Armour and Teece (1980) observed a positive and statistically significant positive partial correlation between research expenditure of petroleum industry firms and their degree of vertical integration. Their regressions cover the 1954–75 period and include only firms with non-zero R&D expenditures. The degree of vertical integration is measured by the number of petroleum industry stages (i.e. crude production, refining, transportation, and marketing) in which a firm participated. Several rather severe econometric problems were encountered in estimating the equations. It should also be noted that Armour and Teece believed that causation runs from vertical integration to innovative behavior rather than, as I have argued, from innovation to vertical integration.

At the other extreme from these examples, the machine tool industry which has not been notable for innovation is notable for the unimportance of vertical integration (see Averitt 1968, pp. 94–8).

NOTES

1. See Canes (1976, p. 108); Lall (1980, p. 206); Malmgren (1961, pp. 413–14).
2. It is assumed that the differential in cost between integrating an operation and purchasing it from an appropriately talented independent firm depends only on its degree of dissimilarity with X production. One could, perhaps, imagine models in which other variables (e.g., scale economies) might also play a role in shaping this differential.
3. See, for example, Bailey and Friedlaender (1982, pp. 1025–8). For ease of exposition I ignore the possibility that $MIPC$ is initially negative due to the existence of economies of scope. See further chapter 13.
4. Perhaps the $MRITC$ curve could also be positively sloped or, alternatively, perhaps there are scale economies in information transmission.
5. Auster and Silver (1976) show how a utility-maximizing entrepreneur would choose his input of time; they also derive necessary conditions for the existence of the backward bending supply curve in terms of elasticities of substitution between entrepreneurship and other factors and the relative share of entrepreneurship.
6. According to Rosenberg (1963, pp. 422–4):

    > Industrialization was characterized by the introduction of a relatively small number of broadly similar productive processes to a large number of industries. This follows from the familiar fact that industrialization in the nineteenth century involved the growing adoption of a metal-using technology employing decentralized sources of power.

If we look at the vertical dimension of productive activity in the sense of the sequence of stages involved in the production of the final product, it appears that in preindustrial economies, skills and techniques tended to be much more specific and tied down to individual vertical sequences than was the case in the industrial economies. The central role in industrial economies of the application of decentralized power sources in the working of metals has meant the employment of similar skills, techniques, and facilities at some of the 'higher' stages of production for a wide range of final products. ... It is because these processes and problems became common to the production of a wide range of disparate commodities that industries which were apparently unrelated from the point of view of the nature and uses of the final product became very closely related (technologically convergent) on a technological basis. ... The intensive degree of specialization which developed in the second half of the nineteenth century owed its existence to a combination of technological convergence plus what Stigler [see chap. 13 below] has called vertical disintegration – that is, a tendency for individual sequences in the production of a final product to be undertaken as separate operations by separate firms.

7. See de Chazeau and Kahn (1959, p. 42); Lall (1980, p. 206).
8. See Nelson and Winter (1982, chapter 5); Penrose (1959, p. 56); Rubin (1973, p. 939).
9. Gort and Klepper (1982) provide an interesting discussion of the spread in the number of firms engaged in producing a new product.
10. Ravenscraft (1983), utilizing Federal Trade Commission survey data for 1975 covering 3,186 'lines of business' (LBs) in 258 4-digit industries, observed that profits rise if the degree of vertical integration for an LB is above average for its industry. The regression coefficients, however, did not achieve statistical significance. There is also some evidence suggesting that the ability of German firms to retain a place among the 100 largest manufacturing companies over the years 1887 to 1907 was strongly related to diversification and vertical integration (Tilly 1982, p. 639). See also section 5.10.
11. Another point relating to agriculture is that the importance of the Japanese 'cultivating landlords' mentioned in section 4.4 diminished in the 1890s and thereafter (Waswo 1977, p. 67).
12. The Japanese *zaibatsu* combines formed in the last quarter of the nineteenth century (see section 4.3) displayed a significant trend

toward the sub-contracting of manufacturing operations beginning in the First World War and the 1920s (Littler 1983, pp. 126–8).
13. The VIC uses the matric framework of the Leontief model basing calculations on national input–output tables.
14. See Boyle (1974, pp. 140–42); Rosenberg (1963, pp. 440–42); Monteverde and Teece (1982, pp. 209–10).

PART II

Applications of the Model of Vertical Integration and Disintegration to Major Themes in Economic History

CHAPTER 6

On Imperialist Enclaves and Dependency

In the later eighteenth century when Colonel Brooke opened a large modern spinning and clothmaking factory in Ireland, he wished to confine himself to the manufacturing end of the business. But within this relatively undeveloped mileau he soon saw the advantage of assuming the additional roles of wholesale and retail merchant (Bowden 1965, p. 43). This quite innocent example serves to focus attention on the role of information impactedness in explaining why foreign firms operating in newly developing areas have so often found it necessary to integrate both backward and forward from their main concerns. The key to this phenomenon is provided by Agmon and Hirsch's (1979, p. 335) observation: 'The costs of communication are usually related to the relative development of the infrastructure in the two countries involved. Where the infrastructure is poor, or even non-existent, as in many LDCs, the costs of communication to the individual firm are likely to be extremely high.' On the other hand, according to the proponents of 'dependency theory', foreign enterprises transformed dynamic and continually evolving societies with sufficient resources for development into static, underdeveloped societies.[1] A number of disparate nineteenth and twentieth century case studies will show, however, that the creation of 'enclaves' is not necessarily a harmful monopolistic imperialistic plot or irreversible, at least by peaceful means.[2]

6.1 PENETRATION BY FOREIGN FIRMS: THE EXAMPLE OF SUGAR

In the early nineteenth century the Liverpool sugar merchant Josias Booker went to British Guiana (later Guyana) and became involved in sugar growing. With the passage of time the firm added a shipping line, wharf and lighterage facilities, integrated forward from sugar into rum production, marketing of sugar and rum and even retailing in the Caribbean and the United Kingdom. By the middle of the twentieth century the firm was sometimes referred to as Booker's Guiana (Channon 1978, pp. 119–20, 126). The large British firm Tate and Lyle began as a sugar refiner, but under the impetus of a rapidly growing market due in part to the emergence of packaged sugar and, later on, a bulk and liquid trade, the firm achieved a notable degree of vertical integration. In 1924 Tate and Lyle began transporting sugar within the United Kingdom. Next, with rapidly growing tonnage, the firm ceased to contract out for lighterage and acquired ownership of lighterage companies. Then in the 1930s it began producing raw sugar in the West Indies. For these plantations the firm produced its own inputs. With the rapid growth of bulk shipment, Tate and Lyle acquired specially designed road tankers for distribution within the United Kingdom and ships for Sugar Line. Finally, the firm acquired engineering firms for the manufacture of sugar machinery and founded a technical service company to serve its refineries as well as its other operations (Beckford 1972, pp. 128–29, 142).

6.2 LEGAL RESTRICTIONS AND CONTRACTUAL SUBSTITUTES FOR VERTICAL INTEGRATION

Sometimes, legal restrictions on vertical integration encourage the adoption of second best contractual solutions to the information impactedness problem. For example, when Del Monte first surveyed the Bajio Valley in Mexico in 1959 it found, in the firm's own words, that 'vegetable production was small and limited to a few crops grown exclusively for the local fresh market' (quoted in Burbach and Flynn 1980, p. 184). But Mexican law prohibited the sale of these lands and placed restrictions on ownership by foreign corporations. Under the circumstances Del Monte could not solve the information impactedness problem by purchasing land and had to rely on a system of contract farming. Under these contracts Del Monte provided the independent, inexperienced local producers with assistance including seeds, special machinery, fertilizers, and technical expertise. In this way the firm succeeded in introducing a variety of new commercial crops that previously had been unimportant in the Mexican diet, including sweet corn, peas, and asparagus. Similarly, given a legal prohibition on foreign ownership of land, the British American Tobacco Company relied on contractual arrangements to introduce the growing of Virginia tobacco into China during the period of the First World War (Allen and Donnithorne 1954a, pp. 53, 170).

6.3 THE EMERGENCE AND RETREAT OF ENCLAVES

On rare occasions the literature permits us a glimpse not only of the rise of enclaves, but of the remainder of the dynamic process including their decline or disintegration in response to economic experience with new goods.[3]

Distributing Consumer Durables in the Philippines

In the early 1950s the electrification of the Philippines sharply increased the demand for appliances including refrigerators, stoves, sewing machines, and television sets. This period was marked by downward sales control: large distributors, independent or often in joint ventures with overseas suppliers, created a fully owned retail network in major urban centers and most provinces. However, beginning in 1963 the fully owned retail outlets were transformed into franchisees. Then in the later 1960s the franchisees were increasingly supplanted by general-line retail stores and independent appliance centers.

The appliance market channel of 1976 in the Phillippines could hardly have been predicted from the vantage point of conditions that prevailed up to about 1965. A system that was well in the hands of the distributors and assemblers was changed to one in which lower channel members gained trade autonomy.... Independent appliance establishments have proliferated as the opportunity to obtain goods from various sources has expanded. Filipinos, many of them former branch managers and franchise holders, operate the majority of these retail outlets. But much of the turnover is now handled by the Chinese. . . . What had developed in the appliance field . . . into a streamlined and fully integrated distribution system has since been transformed into one that is complex, heterogeneous, and nonexclusive, and one in which many channel members are related to one another through pricing rather than formal contractual relations or ownership control. (Dannhaeuser 1981, pp. 584, 586)

The growing importance relative to foreigners of Filipino and Chinese enterprises in the appliance market is fully consistent with the information impaction theory. So also is Dannhaeuser's (p. 587) observation that the observed pattern in many ways is the opposite of what the standard model of market channel development would predict: 'After moving in the expected direction for 15 years, the channel structure dissolved into a more traditional form.' A study by Hill (1982, p. 268) provides a useful postscript. Beginning in the 1970s several distributors of imported appliances entered into manufacturing and since that time local procurement of components, as opposed to in-house production, has been gradually increasing.

Chinese Businessmen in Foreign Trade

The China trade was radically transformed after treaties in 1858 and 1860 gave foreigners direct access to the interior. As Allen and Donnithorne (1954a, p. 37) point out, the Chinese were not in a position to judge which interior products would capture lucrative Western markets – this role fell to Western merchants. They became involved in the organization of the supply of goods required for the export markets and sometimes became directly responsible for the establishment of new industries and the reorganization of existing ones. In addition, these merchants found it expedient to provide many of the ancillary services (banking, foreign exchange, shipping, insurance) left to specialists in Western economies. With the passage of time Chinese import merchants gained in relative importance and several operations were shed by export merchants and taken over by Chinese firms. This, for example, is what happened by the end of the first decade of the twentieth century in the case of pig bristles, one of China's chief export commodities (Allen and Donnithorne 1954a, pp. 31–2, 40, 85).

African Retailers of Western Goods

Vertically integrated foreign-owned firms arose in East, Central, and West Africa in conjunction with the rapid growth of external trade in the later nineteenth and early twentieth centuries. In Central and East Africa trading firms moved into agriculture and mining while, in some cases, firms in the latter industries founded their own marketing and importing organizations (A.G. Hopkins 1976, p. 277). The West African trade in palm-oil and ground nuts (peanuts) had been revolutionized after 1850 but, as Newbury (1969, p. 91) notes, difficulties were encountered on the supply side: 'The history of the European trade with West Africa up till partition [1880–1900] is a long series of attempts to encourage traditional methods of supply to meet new and changing conditions.' Supply problems were intensified by the fact that European firms were generally barred by British and French policy from direct participation in agriculture (see also section 6.2). In the absence of such restrictions on the import side, European firms formed their own wholesale and retail stores throughout the region. Beginning, however, in the 1930s, the picture began to change with the emergence of a pronounced trend toward vertical disintegration. Major importing companies such as the United Africa Company began divesting themselves of retail selling outlets in favor of independent but credit receiving African storekeepers. The latter were frequently former employees of the integrated trading firms (Bauer 1954, pp. 56, 126, 128).

Native Producers in Primary Export Industries

The agricultural history of Malawi (formerly Nyasaland) is quite suggestive (see Kydd and Christiansen, 1982). The years after the establishment of the British Protectorate in 1891 saw the rise of a vigorous export oriented economy in coffee growing and, later on, in cotton and tobacco. Europeans purchased the land of subsistence farmers who were (together with migrants from Mozambique) converted into wage laborers or into tenants providing labor services to the estates under the *thangata* system. The importance of independent export-oriented native farmers began to increase in the 1920s, but cotton and tobacco prices collapsed in the 1930s and many estates were abandoned. Then, in the 1970s, Malawi experienced an extremely sharp growth in tobacco production: from 1965–9 to 1975–9 the production of flue-cured tobacco, the main variety, increased by 886 per cent. This trend was accompanied by the rapid growth of plantations that in many cases expanded into previously uncultivated land, for example in the less populated northern region of Malawi. Once again, with the emergence of opportunities in distant markets, independent farmers were transformed into wage laborers or tenants who agreed to produce and sell tobacco to the estate owner. (The *thangata* or labor services system had been abolished in the closing years of the British administration.) It can be predicted that, just as in the 1920s, growing experience with tobacco markets will be accompanied by a decline in the importance of plantations relative to independent small farmers (see also chapter 7).

In the late nineteenth and early twentieth centuries in Brazil, foreign exporters integrated backward by purchasing coffee plantations and constructing processing and storage facilities (Greenhill 1977, pp. 207–12). But during the first half of the twentieth century in both Brazil and Columbia the exporters retreated from growing, which in relative terms at least was taken over increasingly by small producers (Holloway 1980, pp. 164–8; Safford 1982, pp. 454, 459). At the same time, natives assumed important roles in both marketing and processing.

Prior to 1866 the banana was virtually unknown in Western Europe and the United States. Beginning in 1899 the United Fruit Company (now United Brands) realized the fruit's potential by founding in Central America plantations (see also chapter 10), railways, radio stations, electric plants, ports, a merchant fleet including the first refrigerated vessels in ocean transport, corrugated box manufacturing plants and a national distribution system in the United States. The industry has not experienced vertical disintegration, at least in a very dramatic way. One extenuating circumstance noted in 1958 by May and Plaza (pp. 139, 244; see more recently Ellis 1978, pp. 83ff) is the combination of heavy capital requirements for establishing and maintaining banana acreage with the onslaught of diseases that have necessitated successive shifts in the locale of growing areas. The recreation of pioneering conditions in new growing areas would encourage the perpetuation of vertical integration (see the discussion of the continuously innovating firm in section 5.10 and of bonanza firms in chapter 7). But it is not really true that there have been no signs of vertical disintegration. In his 1978 PhD thesis (1978, p. 94) Ellis informs us that Del Monte, which entered the industry in 1967, 'has followed a rather different policy to that of the Standard Fruit Company [formed in 1926] in terms of the balance between own and purchased fruit production'. Specifically, the balance of the later entering Del Monte is more heavily weighted in terms of purchased fruit. Indeed, even if the difference between Del Monte and Standard Fruit is put aside, there are other indications of changing structure. It would appear that the spread of diseases operated to retard if not reverse a significant trend in the direction of banana growing by independent farmers who, up to the middle of the 1930s, sold their crop to the exporters (May and Plaza 1958, pp. 79, 83, 153, 164). More recently, during the 1960s: (1) United Fruit ceased production in Columbia, Ecuador, and the Dominican Republic and moved entirely into purchase arrangement with separate growers; (2) both United Fruit and Del Monte launched new associated producer programs; (3) taking Costa Rica, Guatemala, Honduras, and Panama together, the proportion of the area worked by independent banana producers rose from 8.5 per cent in 1964 to 34.3 per cent in 1970 (Ellis 1978, pp. 108–11; Arthur et al. 1968, pp. 54–8, 148–9).

Engineering and Electronics in Malaysia and Singapore

In Malaysia it has become common practice for British engineering firms with close links to the primary export industries (tin, rubber, and oil palm) to sub-contract the design and building of milling, mining, and water treatment facilities to local firms owned, usually, by ex-employees of the British firms (Saham 1980, p. 283). This transformation is well illustrated by the history of United Engineers which was founded in the nineteenth century in Singapore as a shipbuilding firm and soon entered the production of rubber machinery and tin dredge building. During the 1950s and 1960s this firm sub-contracted out the erection of dredges and the production of dredge components to local firms. Indeed, locally-owned light engineering firms now account for substantial proportions of the total manufacturing cost of machines and equipment by British engineering firms (Thoburn 1973, pp. 98–101, 106–7, 112). Locally-owned firms also manufacture a variety of materials which serve as inputs for the British firms in the electrical engineering industry (Saham 1980, p. 189). There is also evidence of a transition from in-house manufacture of parts to local buying-out by multinational firms in the export-oriented electronics industry of Singapore. Lim and Fong (1982, p. 592) note this trend toward vertical disintegration has taken place in an atmosphere of minimal government intervention.[4]

6.4 CONCLUDING REMARKS

It is simply wrong to elevate the view that enclaves fail to exert a positive influence on the host country economy to the status of an economic law. More to the point of the present study, it is wrong to advise less developed nations that if they wish to increase their efficiency they must adopt 'regularized', 'systematic', 'simplified', and 'streamlined' approaches to business organization – that is, encourage or force enterprises into a vertically integrated mold. Moreover, the issue with respect to foreign enclaves is neither the 'absence' nor the 'stifling' of local entrepreneurship. Both the integration and disintegration (or market) options are *always* available for a particular operation. The real question, as we have tried to show, is one of expected relative costs. The Chinese, Philippines, Malaysian, and West African examples, taken together with the evolution of agriculture in Brazil, Columbia, Malawi, and (I believe) Central America, nicely illustrate how, with the passage of time, the relative costs tend to change in such a way that the importance in a given industry of foreign enterprise decreases relative to that of host country entrepreneurs.

NOTES

1. See Austen (1981); Dos Santos (1970); Myrdal (1957, pp. 23–32, 57–60).
2. In the economic development literature the term foreign enclave usually refers to a firm (or firms) native to an economically advanced nation that produces and exports primary products from a less developed country. Given, however, our interest in the emergence in less developed countries of independently managed firms, it is natural to extend the meaning of enclave to encompass all vertically integrated foreign enterprises.
3. Our focus is on the decline of foreign enclaves via vertical disintegration. It should be understood that economic experience will also result in import substitution – that is, foreign enterprises will find it cheaper to purchase certain inputs from independent host country firms than to continue importing them (see Thoburn 1977, p. 42).
4. McAleese and McDonald (1978) found that new foreign-owned firms in Ireland tend to increase the share of Irish materials (raw materials, components, and packaging) with the passage of time. In some developing countries the economic forces promoting vertical disintegration have been strengthened by legal factors. Thus, for instance, in the Taiwanese machinery sector sub-contracting has emerged in several branches where foreign capital plays an important role, namely sewing machines, agricultural equipment, and automobiles. However, as Amsden (1977, p. 223) points out, this trend is due not only to the 'willingness of some prime producers to surround themselves with a constellation of satellites', but to the fact that 'foreign firms and joint ventures in the above named branches have been forced to sub-contract by law.' Government pressures have also played some role in the shift since 1975 of international hotel chains operating in less developed countries from ownership to management contracts. Note, however, that this trend is also observable in the developed countries in which such pressures are absent (McQueen 1983, p. 143).

CHAPTER 7

The Rises and Falls of Manors, Latifundia and Bonanzas

7.1 MEDIEVAL ENGLAND

It is convenient to begin a consideration of the vexed questions of manorialism, serfdom, feudalization, defeudalization, and refeudalization by considering the experience of the black monks of the autonomous houses in northern England. Prior to the thirteenth century when production for distant markets was unimportant, the latter played only a negligible role in the exploitation of their estates. However, beginning in the thirteenth century with the significant growth of urban (e.g. London) and international (e.g. Flanders) markets for grain and wool, the monks took demesne land under direct control as leases fell due and cultivated grain and raised sheep and cattle for the market. Prominent examples of this trend include the overseas grain and wool shipments of the Christ Church and Canterbury manors (Knowles 1948, pp. 33, 364; Miller and Hatcher 1978, p. 225).

These events lead easily into the fundamental question in medieval English agricultural organization: the choice between labor dues (or hired labor) and money (or in-kind) rents in the cultivation of the manorial demesne. Fenoaltea (1975, p. 695) has put forward the hypothesis that the advantage of farming the demesne with labor services 'attached specifically to the exercise of authority over the labor force' by the lord, which 'might be considered a means to increase output by imposing the use of superior technique.' However, seeking the benefit of authority in differential technical expertise – that is, in production functions, seems to run counter to the evidence. Kerridge (1973, p. 52) notes quite reasonably that:

Common-field agriculture was not necessarily inferior to that in undivided or severalty ground. As long as the demesne was cultivated by tenants' services, or in so far as it was, the skills employed there and in the common fields were almost identical. In each, the general plan of management, the field courses, crop rotation, implements, livestock, and everything else were much the same. The tenants could hardly have shown more skill on the demesne than on their own holdings.

Miller and Hatcher (1978, p. 224) add that demesne and tenant farming were biased to just about the same extent toward cereal growing. But the upward surge in demesne agriculture and labor services in the thirteenth century, culminating in some estates in the phase of 'high farming', does seem quite consistent with differential expertise with respect to the potential of distant markets. To say that the failure of the ordinary farmer to participate in commercial relations is 'a result of serfdom' (meaning labor services?[1]) is to reverse the direction of causation. Predictably, given the absence of any pronounced economies of scale, the period prior to the Black Death in 1349 witnessed the gradual abandonment of labor services in favor of the renting out of the demesne to independent cultivators.[2] The hypothesis that the lord's authority compensated for differentials in market information rather than in technical expertise seems to be consistent with another body of evidence as we shall see below.[3]

7.2 ORGANIZATIONAL TRENDS IN GRECO-ROMAN AGRICULTURE[4]

During the second to first centuries BCE (Before the Common Era) the comparative advantage of large parts of the Roman Republic became such that domestic cereal production declined sharply in favor of imported grains from Egypt, North Africa and Sicily. The Roman countryside moved toward pasturage and the production of wool and meat for the newly affluent urban centers of which Rome itself was the supreme example. This transition was accompanied by the formation of large ranches in Latium, Etruria and the southern parts of Italy. Livestock raising, of course, is considerably less labor intensive than cereal production and it is probable that the rural population decreased significantly at this time.[5] In Campania, whose gravelly soil was well suited to olives and vines, the small grain producer gave way to wine and oil plantations which supplied the new markets in the urban centers as well as in Gaul, Germany and India.[6] The latter plantations were worked by slaves or, more precisely, as Yeo (1952, p. 328) explains, by Syrian slaves who were 'adept in the refined art of handling plants and of transplanting, grafting, and pruning vines, a knowledge indispensable to successful viticulture'.[7] So the labor force knew all about the technical aspects of wine and oil production but was, of course, totally unaware of the market opportunities for Italian products.[8] This knowledge was supplied by the slavemasters, the plantation owners.

But the technical expertise factor provides an answer to the 'puzzling' question posed by Keith Hopkins (1978, pp. 10, 108–9): 'Why did the rich not make use of free wage laborers instead of buying slaves out of capital? . . . Slavery was by no means an obvious solution to the elite's need for agricultural labor. [Even if somewhat exaggerated in the earlier literature] the extrusion of free peasants created a large pool of landless or underemployed citizens. The rich could have employed them to work their estates as tenants or day-wage laborers.' Rathbone (1981, p. 14) contends that slave labor was not 'more economic' in this type of agriculture than free. However, while his attempt at quantification deserves applause, Rathbone's supporting calculations are misleading because he utilizes wages for unskilled labor when, as his own quote from Columella (fn. 19, p. 13) makes clear, a decent 'vintnor' came quite expensive. The point that Hopkins missed is that the Roman landlord was hardly likely to bear the cost of importing skilled and, therefore, highly valuable Syrian workers unless he could count on controlling (owning) their future labor services. Such control was exactly what the institution of slavery provided: the imported vintnor was not legally free upon arrival to accept the highest wage offer.

During the first century CE the plantation system with its slave labor was replaced not by labor services or even by wage labor, but by independent farmers who rented the land on which they grew olives and vines. It is traditional to explain this startling transition in terms of an alleged decrease in the supply of slaves. As Garnsey (1980, pp. 39–40) explains: 'The issue of the slave supply is crucial. It is regularly stated that the supply of slaves dwindled after the reign of Augustus and that landowners were in consequence forced to lease more of their land to tenant-farmers.' (Why they could not have hired free labor is not explained.) Garnsey continues that it 'still seems necessary to insist that the truth of this statement cannot be established with reference to the sources. We are told more of tenancy under the Empire than under the Republic, but this may be quite by chance.' But while direct evidence of a decline in the supply of slaves is absent, this does not at all imply that the more frequent references to tenancy are a matter of chance.[9] The information impaction hypothesis predicts that with the passage of time, knowledge regarding markets for wine and oil (and technical expertise as well) would penetrate to the grassroots of the Italian farming population with the consequence that more costly production by large plantations employing shirking labor (slave or free) would be replaced by independent wine and oil producers.[10] (At this point Rathbone's calculations come closer to the mark.) Petit (1976, p. 82) concludes that: 'Cultivation passed from the hands of a few big operators to those of many smaller ones, yet still within the framework of large-scale capitalism. Classical estate management, based on great estates worked by slaves under the orders of a *vilicus* . . . was in a rapid decline. . . . Estates were divided up into small units entrusted to tenant farmers.'

In evaluating the contribution of the information impaction hypothesis to our understanding of the evolution of Roman agricultural organization, the following points should be recognized. First, with the passage of time and the diffusion of knowledge regarding market opportunities, small farmers were apparently both *willing* and *able* to gain access to whatever capital was necessary to participate in the production of olives and grapes for the market. This suggests that the origins of land consolidation and farming with dependent labor should not be sought in the inability of free persons to acquire capital. Admittedly these investments were not insignificant. Viticulture involves the continuous application of skilled labor while the olive requires a great deal of care in the five years before it is transplanted and does not yield a full harvest for about twenty years. Further, in the formative stages of the industry a market-oriented producer might have found it efficient to acquire presses, crushers, and storage facilities.[11] Second, if the emerging small businessmen were drawn from the ranks of the slaves or their descendants, the vertical disintegration trend cannot be attributed to the diffusion of technical knowledge. The slaves had this knowledge to begin with. If they were drawn from the ranks of outsiders (the displaced free persons or their descendants), that is, from the ranks of persons without production experience, then, once again, vertical disintegration cannot be explained by the diffusion of technical knowledge. Businessmen from outside the industry could have learned the production functions of olives and vines only *after* they entered and participated in production.

The light cast by our hypothesis seems to penetrate back to Greece in the seventh century BCE, although in this case the evidence is so scanty that it is difficult to draw a coherent picture. At that time, according to Woodhouse (1938, pp. 144–50, 154–5), the emerging pattern of comparative advantage favored the production in Attica of olives and wine for export as opposed to cereals for domestic consumption. In Greece, as possibly in Rome prior to the second century BCE vines and olive trees were grown for subsistence and for sale in local markets, but were not of high quality and undoubtedly represented a small proportion of agricultural output.[12] The result was an agricultural revolution in which land ownership (or at least control) passed from small independent farmers into the hands of more worldly-wise aristocrats who were willing to undertake the required investments. My impression is that the previously independent farmers provided labor services in the legal status of sharecroppers.[13] Foreign slaves were imported to augment the labor supply.

Unlike the case of Rome it does not seem possible to gauge the relative importance of these labor supply adjustments. In any event, Attic wine and oil found new and enlarged markets in the Black Sea area, Sicily, Etruria, Asia Minor, Egypt, the Aegean islands and, of course, in Greece proper.[14] Later, during the seventh and sixth centuries, many 'tenants' (and former slaves?) having become familiar with the markets for grapes and olives took loans from landowners and exporters and became independent cultivators.[15] The Greek pattern is relatively obscure, but it seems similar to that observed later in Rome and, for that matter, in medieval England. Once again the focus on information impaction appears to provide new insights into agricultural phenomena. In the Greek case, however, it does not seem possible to distinguish between the effects of the diffusion of market knowledge as opposed to technical knowledge.

7.3 THE 'SECOND SERFDOM' IN GERMANY AND POLAND

Starting in the middle of the sixteenth century with the emergence of new markets in Western Europe including Portugal, Spain, and Italy, the cultivation of grain (especially rye) spread throughout northeastern Germany and Poland.[16] During this period of 'second serfdom' or 'refeudalization' many small independent farmers were replaced by large wage-paying or labor service-using estates.[17] The latter estates exported through such ports as Königsberg and Gdansk (Danzig). Note with respect to Fenoaltea's hypothesis that the Polish scholars are generally agreed that the methods of agricultural production on the demesne-serf estates were similar to those on peasant land.[18] Nevertheless, Kamiński (1975, p. 267) notes that 'in place after place peasants were finding it impossible to keep up with high money rents.' Then he adds:

For some reason, perhaps because of economies of scale relating to transport or marketing, peasants could not consistently take advantage of high grain prices to convert their surpluses into cash. As a result, they had to surrender some of the risks and opportunities of surplus production to the manor in return for greater security in the form of a hereditary plot of land for which they paid nominal rent and heavy *robot* [labor service] obligations. . . . An illustration of the resulting interdependence between lord and peasants is the fact that at the very time when peasant flight constituted the greatest disaster for a landlord, the most effective threat against refractory peasants was eviction.

The explanation for the switch from money rents to labor services does not, however, lie in mysterious 'economies of scale' but in the information impaction problem. The great magnates in the hinterland of Gdansk were in a better position to understand the problems and potentials of the export trade than their less worldly-wise neighbors (Maczak 1968, p. 88). While some Polish and Royal Prussian peasants must have produced grain for export, it must be noted that the demesnes played a disproportionate role[19] and that the decline in the number of independent farmers was evidently most pronounced in the Polish areas which had been the least market-oriented (Mayhew 1973, p. 140). Indeed, as predicted by our theory, the market involvement of small farmers was most prominent in the immediate vicinity of Gdansk and other towns (Maczak 1968, pp. 95–6). Equally predictable is the fact that large manorial estates failed to evolve in southwestern Germany which played no important role in the export of grain (Nichtweiss 1979, p. 102).

Postan's (1973, p. 334) discussion of the *'Bauernlegen'* is rather confused, but in the end he admits that 'there is no denying that the main reason why the *Bauernlegen* occurred . . . is that the corn-trade exports were growing . . . and that landlords could not exploit the full potentialities of the trade so long as peasants owned much of the arable and withheld their labor. In this way one of the most tragic paradoxes of European history came to be enacted. In conventional histories, trade is often treated as a liberating force and as a solvent of serfdom and feudal power; in this particular instance it enhanced the forces of resurgent feudalism.' But this episode was neither paradoxical nor unique. Neither was it necessarily tragic unless we insist, contrary to the wishes of the 'peasants' themselves, on making independent farming an absolute value.

A different explanation for the emergence of labor services has recently been put forward by Millward. Prior to enserfment in the sixteenth century, Millward (1982, p. 518) explains, the market provided a means whereby: 'Peasant productivity ... is motivated by other peasants. If a peasant lies about what he is able to produce – and therefore what he is able to pay in rent – other peasants stand ready to take up his holding.' But enserfment, according to Millward, involved *both* forced immobility of labor and the destruction of the rental market for land. In the absence of the market, close monitoring of labor services provided eastern European landlords with a relatively economical means by which they might acquire knowledge of potential output levels.[20] Perhaps. On the other hand, arguably more efficient techniques come easily to mind. For example, why did not the landlords rely on historical (or even experimental) data on output (or rentals) for their lands? Surely there were no great changes in the agricultural arts to invalidate such data. More basically, the rental market certainly did not disappear in manorial England and it is questionable whether it did even in eastern Europe or, for that matter, whether forcible enserfment was really as important as Millward suggests.[21] Notice that while Millward cites evidence of serf-sales, he adds that these transactions are dwarfed by the reports of usage of free wage labor. He considers the question of why some agricultural labor was not enserfed to be outside the scope of his paper. We are told that 'by the second half of the eighteenth century in East Elbian Germany and Prussia a considerable part of estate labor (at least half on some estates) came from cottagers, with a garden and a customary wage, as well as by wholly landless day laborers' and, indeed, that 'it has been estimated that in East Prussia as early as 1700 the 69,231 peasants with holdings were outnumbered by 72,611 landless farm laborers' (Millward 1982, pp. 537, 542).

Beginning in the eighteenth century and continuing into the nineteenth, eastern European landlords switched over from labor services to money rents (Kula 1976, p. 150; Topolski 1981, p. 399). This is, of course, the kind of reversal predicted by our theory stressing the gradual penetration of knowledge of the new markets to the grass roots of the society.[22] Some Marxist-oriented economic historians (for example Brenner 1976, p. 52), however, have sought to attribute such undulations in agricultural organization to 'class struggle' or, more specifically, to assumed rather than independently demonstrated differences or changes 'in the balance of class forces between the peasants and the lords'. Topolski (1981, pp. 392–3) properly dismisses this sort of sleight of hand, but his own attempt to explain both 'refeudalization' in the sixteenth century and 'defeudalization' in the eighteenth century in terms of landlord activism generated by 'widening gaps' or 'contradictions' between their 'incomes and needs' amounts to explaining a phenomenon by itself. Millward (1982, p. 538) does not attempt to explain the rising importance of money rents relative to labor services beginning in the eighteenth century. (The freeing of the serfs in eastern Europe took place mainly in the nineteenth century.) He does, however, cite remarks concerning the difficulties of estimating the 'maximum quantities of land and labor time to leave to the peasant for his subsistence' and the consequent 'gradual encroachment of peasant land to which it led, as well as the surplus manpower that it sometimes left behind on peasant land.' Clearly evidence of this kind provides no explanation of the decline of 'serfdom' and, in addition, it serves to undermine Millward's explanation for the rise of labor services in the sixteenth century.

7.4 THE EXPERIENCE OF THE US: PLANTATIONS IN THE SOUTH, BONANZAS AND CATTLE KINGS IN THE WEST

The invention of the cotton gin in 1793 revolutionized southern agriculture by making it commercially feasible to grow seedy short-staple cotton in the Piedmont or upland areas of the Carolinas and Georgia. Previously, easily seeded long-staple cotton had been produced for the market, but it grew well only in a rather restricted area consisting of some islands off the coast of Georgia and South Carolina as well as certain coastal lowlands. Upland grain farmers, on the other hand, had been growing short-staple cotton on a miniscule scale with a small fraction being sold and the rest being used by the farm households to make a coarse cloth (Cohn 1956, p. 18). English factory owners, perceiving the enormous potential demand for cheap cotton fabrics to replace woollens and linens, looked forward eagerly to increased cotton imports. But what, after all, did upland farmers know of English factories and the demand for cotton cloth? Understandably, they hesitated to make the required investments including terracing their hilly land. Instead, numerous small farmers took advantage of rising land prices by selling out to large planters and moving on or becoming day laborers (Gates 1960, pp. 9, 136). Faced with the exodus of the former small farmers and the labor-intensive nature of cotton cultivation, the newly formed plantations imported slaves in large numbers. Cotton production soared from about 3,000 bales in 1790 to about 209,000 bales in 1815 and still prices tended to rise (Gates 1960, pp. 7–8).

The years that followed saw the expansion of large cotton plantations on to the fertile soil of the lower South. Meanwhile, the relative importance of large plantations was declining in the older cotton growing areas. Census data for 1850 and 1860 presented by Wright (1976, p. 337) show that, excluding the alluvial region, the share of cotton output produced by plantations with 51 or more slaves declined from 35 to 24 per cent.[23] This trend is predictable given the monumental shirking problem and the declining importance of the information impaction problem with the passage of time.[24]

Events in the great unsettled West of the United States in the second half of the 1870s are also consistent with our theory. Prior to 1870 only the spring variety of wheat which yielded a dark, inferior flour could be grown in the area, but then a Minneapolis miller, Edmund N. La Croix, developed the middings purifier which eliminated the objection to the product. A number of eastern businessmen, including railroad officials who had become aware of the commercial potential of the region, purchased large tracts of land in the Red River Valley of North Dakota and Minnesota. But who was to farm this land? Apparently small independent farmers were unwilling to offer appropriate rental payments, so the businessmen–landlords decided to farm the land themselves. This was accomplished by means of so-called bonanza farms – that is, large farms run by hired managers and worked by wage laborers.

Beginning in 1879 and 1880 the attention given by the

media to the profitability of the bonanza farms contributed to a rapid influx of small farmers. By the later 1880s and 1890s the Red River Valley had become the nation's leading wheat region. By this time, however, as Fite (1966, pp. 85–6) reports, the type of agricultural organization represented by bonanza farms was declining as many of the large property holders were selling out to small farmers or renting their land to individual operators on a share basis. Why was the large operator crowded out by small wheat producers? The answer seems to be that large-scale wheat production by means of hired labor raised costs, with the result that once his informational advantage was dissipated – that is, once the commercial opportunities of the Red River Valley and, indeed, of the entire 'Great West' were widely recognized – bonanza farming was doomed.[25] Also during this period, but some 2,000 miles away, bonanza wheat farming experienced a similar evolution in California's Central Valley where 'the main topic of conversation were the rain and the Liverpool market' (Fite 1966, pp. 86, 171–4). Note also the evolution of Montana's corporation wheat farms of the 1920s.

Earlier in the 1840s and 1850s, when the cattle trails of Texas were still unknown, pioneering cattle kings rode the prairies of central Illinois. Several perceptive cattle feeders and drovers including Isaac Funk, Jacob Strawn, and John T. Alexander recognized that while central Illinois lacked the transportation facilities necessary for extensive wheat growing, it possessed an abundance of tall, sweet grass and was well placed for raising cattle purchased from isolated prairie farmers for driving to the cities of the eastern seaboard as well as the rising livestock centers in Chicago and St. Louis (Bogue 1963, pp. 86, 92–3). Apparently, the corn-growing operation did not keep pace with the expansion of cattle feeding which was reinforced by the introduction of heavier cattle of improved breed, for the cattle kings gave up their previous practice of purchasing grain and purchased large tracts of land on which they grew their own corn (Bogue 1963, p. 94; Gates 1960, p. 194). But, as Gates (1948, p. 411) reports, the cattle kings encountered difficulties hiring reliable conscientious workers: 'The hired hands were migratory workers who were undependable, drank heavily, sometimes shirked their work, and were frequently in trouble with the law.' Meanwhile, applications for tenant holdings became more numerous. By 1865 the area had experienced a transition from bonanza farms toward independent corn-growing: 'The proprietors divided their large fields and pastures into small units which they rented to tenants on a crop-share basis, or they provided the farm equipment and seed and paid the tenants seven cents a bushel for all the corn they raised' (Gates 1960, p. 194).

7.5 CONCLUDING REMARKS

One important lesson for economists of the historical evidence presented in this chapter, in chapter 6 and in section 4.8 (on sugar beet growing) is that they must be wary of assuming that the emergence of large farming units reflects the magnitude or even the existence of economies of scale. Serious errors can result if due allowance is not made for age, in terms of commercial time, of the product.

NOTES

1. The term 'serfdom' is usually associated with forced immobility of 'unpaid' labor. All too often in discussions of manorialism this condition is simply *assumed*, not demonstrated by recourse to the evidence. Blum (1961, p. 7) reminds us that 'there were periods in serfdom's history when the bondman had the right to leave his holding, after giving notice to his lord, whereupon he became a free man.' In any event, as Millward (1982, pp. 513–14) points out, force alone cannot explain why the landlord chose labor services and not cash or crop rent: 'Why not extract the profit from forced immobility as a rent? Why is demesne labor associated with enserfment?' A perfectly good question and solution. Note that Millward here seems to identify 'enserfment' with labor services.
2. Miller and Hatcher (1978, p. 223). Chao (1983, pp. 202–3) has suggested that if population growth drives the marginal product of labor below the subsistence level, a shift from 'latifundia' to tenancy will be encouraged. His argument may be summarized as follows: 'In that case, the subsistence cost forms a wage floor for farms employing full-time workers and those farms must stop

hiring at the point where the marginal product of labor is equal to the subsistence wage.... The redundancy of surplus labor will be absorbed by tenant farmers who have the obligation to support their family members. [Consequently] the marginal product of labor in tenant farming is considerably below the subsistence level.... Accordingly, the marginal product of land under [latifundia and tenancy respectively] tends to shift in the opposite way.' Aside, however, from the factual question of whether the marginal product of labor is really below the subsistence level, Chao's argument is logically flawed. The redundant workers could be employed by the (more efficient?) latifundia at wages below the subsistence level with the deficiency made up by 'welfare payments' from tenants who, by Chao's assumption, have an obligation to support their relatives. In short, given all Chao's assumptions, it still does not follow that all 'redundant labor' must be absorbed by tenant farms.

3. But for Roemer (1982, pp. 93–4) the proposition that 'the Lord possessed certain skills or abilities to organize manor life without which the serfs would have been worse off' is one that might be put forward by a 'feudal ideologue'. The reply of a 'new class ideologue' might be: 'the claim is rebutted by Brenner (1976), and will not be further discussed here.' In spite of Marx, many Neo-Marxists fear to attribute any positive features to 'feudalism'.

4. I would like to thank Chester G. Starr for his very helpful comments on an earlier version of this section.

5. Yeo (1948). This is not to say, however, that small farmers disappeared. For a summary of the archaeological evidence for Etruria, see Potter (1979, pp. 95–6, 123–7).

6. White (1970, pp. 226, 229). The Campanian estate that Cato the Elder (d. 149 BCE) had his slaves plant with olive trees and vines previously supported seventeen wheat-growing families (Lévy 1967, p. 67). On exports, see Yeo (1952, pp. 334–41); Frederiksen (1970–71). The conclusions regarding exports are based largely on the finding of Campanian amphorae used as wine and oil containers.

7. See also Rathbone (1981). The importance of Syrian slaves in Campania is supported by sporadic literary and archaeological evidence. 'At Minturnae they [Syrian slaves] and slaves of Anatolian origin constituted about 67 percent of the total slave population.... It has been ... shown that in and around the city of Pompeii ... the number of Syrians and Anatolians was sufficiently large to justify Juvenal's growl about the Syrian

Orontes flowing into the Tiber.... Many Pompeian amphorae are stamped with Greek or Latin words in Greek form, indicating how strongly the Greek speaking Oriental element was represented in Campanian slavery. One of these amphorae turned up in Switzerland, another in Rome' (Yeo 1952, p. 328).
8. It might be suggested that if the slaves were in fact technically proficient, that supervision costs could be reduced by employing them as 'hutted slaves' with a rent obligation in kind. Perhaps, but as noted in note 13, the rental option raises supervision problems of its own. More basically, it would misallocate a scarce resource for slave owners to have slaves technically proficient in wine and olive growing spend part of their working time producing subsistence goods (e.g. cereals) for themselves.
9. With respect to the question of slave supply, Finley (1973, p. 86) points to the 'curious assumption' that 'Germans, who remained outside the empire, were somehow unsatisfactory as slaves unlike the other "barbarian" peoples who had been suitable for many preceding centuries, to the Greeks as to the Romans. The assumption is not only unsupported in the ancient sources, it is belied, for example by the slaving activities in the course of the wars with the Goths.'
10. A passage in Columella's writings (quoted in White 1970, p. 351) provides eloquent testimony to the dimensions of the shirking problem. In the event that the owner is not in a position to undertake regular supervision he should, Columella urges, rent his land out to free tenants. See also Finley's (1973, p. 113) remarks. The shirking problem would swamp any meager economies of scale in vine and olive growing.
11. See Frederiksen (1970–71, pp. 350–51); White (1970, chapter ix and pp. 425–7). Cato the Elder is known to have had an olive-crusher weighing as much as 3,000 pounds shipped to his estate by ox-team wagon from Pompeii some one hundred miles away. Posto, an excavated estate at Francolise near Capua that was probably founded between 120 and 80 BCE featured storage rooms, several cement-lined vats used in the separation of olive oil, and large *dolia* set into the ground, perhaps for wine fermentation (Potter 1979, pp. 126–7). It seems probable, however, that as the industry matured the pressing and crushing functions were more and more taken over by specialized firms. On the contracting out of such services, see Frederiksen (1970–71, p. 350).
12. French (1964, p. 22). Interspersing vines, olive trees, and gardens among rows of grain met the essential consumption

needs of the farm household while the diversified crop portfolio provided a hedge against yield variability, notorious for olives (White 1970, p. 48). These benefits were secured, however, at the cost of reduced yields (Semple 1931, p. 400). Efficient adaptation to changed market opportunities required the Greeks and later the Romans massively to redirect their resources in the direction of specialization in wine and oil of relatively high quality. The olive is perhaps not native to Italy while the vine is met from time immemorial. Nevertheless, the evidence suggests that the production of high quality Italian wine (e.g. Campanian Falernian) dates from the period of declining cereal cultivation (see Oliver 1907, pp. 13, 114–15).

13. The providers of labor services have less incentive to shirk under share contracts than under wage contracts. On the other hand, in their zeal for higher incomes, sharecroppers (workers) may abuse the landlord's (employer's) land, vine and tree stock, and capital goods (see Silver and Auster in appendix 2; Jaynes 1982, p. 362). In the plantation South of the United States, for example, the payment on a share basis 'tempted the overseers into exploiting the soil and overworking the slaves, but the most careful masters early in the nineteenth century shifted their overseers to a salary basis' (Robert 1952, p. 62). In cases where the opportunism problem is not severe, the innovating landlords might seek to reduce contract enforcement costs by relying on sharecroppers rather than on wage laborers. The problem of abuse is mitigated when the sharecropper owns his animal stock or implements or, as (apparently) in the Greek case, retains legal ownership of his land.

14. See French (1964, pp. 25, 43–4, 50). The evidence for exports is mainly archaeological, taking the form of Attic pottery suitable for carrying wine and oil (see, for example, Starr 1977, pp. 68–70).

15. Von Fritz (1943, pp. 30–31). According to Von Fritz, 'ancient tradition leaves no doubt that the practice of selling hektemors [small Athenian farmers] into slavery became more and more frequent in the second half of the seventh and sixth century, that is, just at the time when the export of olive oil from Athens experienced its greatest expansion.' I would surmise that the explanation is that at this time many farmers pledged their bodies (as was possible in antiquity, see Silver 1983, chapter 5) in order to acquire loans to buy or raise olive or vine stock. Contrary to what is usually assumed, an increase in the number of debt-slaves may reflect not economic depression, but an

expanding economy in which an increased number of persons are borrowing in order to invest. Naturally, some of these investors are bound to fail due to inability to run a business or bad luck. Even if these losers constituted a small minority of all borrowers, the total number of persons falling into slavery might well rise.

16. Maczak (1968); Makkai (1975, pp. 237–8); Malowist (1981); Mayhew (1973, pp. 139–40); Nichtweiss (1979, p. 108).
17. Maczak (1968, pp. 94–5); Malowist (1959, p. 186); Mayhew (1973, p. 139); Topolski (1981, pp. 379–80). Topolski (pp. 396–7) adds that the demesne farms also innovated in the cattle market.
18. Kula (1976, pp. 116–18); Maczak (1968, p. 96); Mayhew (1973, p. 169); Millward (1982, p. 515).
19. Maczak (1968, p. 88) provides some quantitative evidence: 'The data about sending grain by the Vistula River surely overstress the share of the surplus originating from large estates: middle size estates and the smaller ones certainly could better sell their grain on local markets (it can be easily proven from eighteenth century sources). But the share of the big landlords in the export of grain was several times higher than it should result from the percentage of land belonging to them in the 3rd quarter of the sixteenth century.' The discussions of Klíma (1979, p. 60) and Kula (1976, p. 149) also suggest in a qualitative manner the preponderance of demesnes. Millward (1982, p. 544), on the other hand, citing Zytkowicz's (1963) tithe data, raises the possibility that demesnes were not preponderant, but he is willing to grant that in the Plock episcopate in Masovia (in central Poland) 'the percentage of grain output accounted for by the commercial crop, rye, rose during 1595–1650 proportionately more on demesne land than on peasant land, it did nevertheless rise on peasant land from 60 to 70 percent.' Zytkowicz (p. 106), however, cautions that 'we cannot be certain that the structure of the tithes accurately reflects the structure of total production. The amounts of actual grain sown would certainly be a better indication of what a peasant intended to produce, but unfortunately no data are available on this subject.' This is an important point, as the structure of tithes may well reflect the preferences of those collecting them – that is, the relatively worldly-wise and wealthy. In addition, the Plock episcopal estates of Masovia were within easy reach of the Vistula and, therefore Gdansk. Zytkowicz (p. 106) also notes, consistently with our theory, that the 1650 inventory 'continually mentions

peasant fields which were ploughed up by the . . . landlord.'
20. The landlord might acquire knowledge of production possibilities by monitoring effort on peasant holdings. 'There would be no expansion of demesne or labor services. . . . But . . . with no other change in the basic characteristics of the peasant holding and cultivation supervision of all the labor time of the peasant would be necessary even though a large part of the resultant produce would accure to the peasant. A saving in supervision time would therefore be made if some of the inputs to production were clearly marked off as due to the lord so that only those inputs would need to be supervised' (Millward 1982, p. 528). The problem here is that the serf would be more inclined to shirk on demesne land whose product belonged wholly to the landlord than on a peasant holding whose output belonged partially to himself.
21. Millward (1982, p. 525) tells us that: 'The legislation to this effect largely of the sixteenth century, is not always a good guide. . . . During the fifteenth century [note: estate formation is primarily a matter of the period beginning in the middle of the sixteenth century] the nobility were active in preventing peasants from leaving their estates, in pressing the towns and others for the return of runways, and in flouting contractual arrangements for labor services. *There is evidence in the sixteenth century of nobles buying out peasant holdings at an "estimated" price prior to any legal authorization of this practice*' (italics added). Indeed, Millward (p. 527) provides evidence of the presence of rental payments by eastern European 'enserfed peasants' throughout the sixteenth, seventeenth, and eighteenth centuries. Finally, if as Millward (pp. 524–5) maintains, the previously independent farmers were forcibly 'prevented from leaving their holdings without the lord's permission, deprived of all rights in the location, quantity, and disposition of their labor time, and deprived of all property in their holdings', Why did the landlords meet only 'very feeble resistance by the peasants' (Kula 1976, p. 115)? This is not how humans (even "peasants") react to such unprecedented and arbitrary actions.
22. Another point to be reckoned with is that by the end of the eighteenth century, Polish grain exports had fallen precipitously from their level at the beginning of the century (Kula 1976, p. 115).
23. During the same period the relative importance of the largest plantations was increasing in the alluvial area (Wright 1976, p. 319). This can, perhaps, be understood in terms of the

recreation of pioneering conditions, including the construction and maintenance of levees.

24. A lower limit on the size of cotton growing firms is provided by the existence of economies of scale, including those allegedly due to the gang system. Actually, the latter can probably be traced back to economies in the supervision process. Similar economies from grouping workers have been noted on Indian tea plantations (Buchanan 1934, p. 65). The importance of this factor remains the subject of an intense econometric debate, see most recently Fogel and Engerman (1980); Schaeffer and Schmitz (1982); Wright (1978, pp. 74–87). Shirking problems were magnified in the Piedmont by the hilly terrain and the scattering of fields as compared to the flat, compact fields of the Mississippi bottom lands (Kirkland 1951, p. 165). On the other hand, the importance of the shirking problem is probably not as great for cotton as for tobacco, where very close supervision is required to produce a high grade crop (see Robert 1952, p. 61).

25. Fite (1966, p. 97) notes that 'the early success of bonanza farming in the Red River Valley advertised Dakota as a paradise for wheat growers.'

CHAPTER 8

The Putting-Out System and the Development of Capitalism

The emergence of the putting-out or domestic system, a much discussed industrial phenomenon, in which the merchant made the necessary investment in the acquisition of raw materials and then put them out to (more or less) geographically dispersed producers, is quite consistent with our emphasis on the information impaction problem. Under this hybrid form of industrial organization, the strategic decision of what to produce was shifted to an outsider, while managing and manual labor remained united in the hands of the artisan (Freudenberger and Redlich 1964, p. 378). Correspondingly, piece rates replaced simple market-type exchanges. As Millward (1981, p. 24) firmly notes: 'The transaction between worker and merchant was not a market transaction in the product – for the worker did not own his output. . . . Rather, the system had some affinities to the characteristics of the "firm".'[1] In Western Europe during the sixteenth to eighteenth centuries the putting-out system, predictably, became especially prominent in newly emerging export centers and products. However, it will be shown that it is inappropriate to speak here of unilinear stages of industrial evolution.

The Florentine woollen industry, for example, which sold mostly in the distant Levant, was organized on the basis of the putting-out system (de Roover 1974, pp. 91–2). The guild system in which artisans produced for direct sale to consumers persisted in cities such as Cologne and Aachen, while the newer export-oriented industries located themselves in the surrounding countryside and employed rural labor in a putting-out system. In the eighteenth century vigorous growth in the colonial and industrial demand for linen encouraged the spread of the putting-out system in such exporting areas as Brittany, Silesia, Westphalia, Flanders (which exported mainly to Spain and her colonies) as well as Scotland, and Ireland (De Vries 1976, pp. 94–8, 103–4). In England, in the later eighteenth century, the move toward the putting-out system was associated with a shift, within a given (even) 'stagnant' production technology, from the older, heavier woollens (and leather products) to lighter, brighter worsteds and other new draperies demanded by the rising urban middle class at home and on the Continent (Coleman 1973, pp. 5–11; Millward 1981, p. 29; Wilson 1957, p. 106). (The putting-out system was also evident in the middle of the eighteenth century among the brass and copper workers of Birmingham. The latter city, quite consistently with our stress on information impactedness, was the most important center of the industry and its products were exported throughout England and to the Continent (H. Hamilton 1926, p. 122). The invention of the fly shuttle in 1733 drastically increased the demand for yarn from Rhineland weavers of cotton and fustians. To cope with this upsurge, merchants converted former spinners of linen and wool to working on imported cotton. This conversion was, of course, largely accomplished by means of the putting-out system (Adelmann 1969, p. 85).

Several cross-sectional and time-series comparisons serve to strengthen this line of argument, while casting doubt on alternative theories of putting-out stressing the absence of working captial or improved quality control (Millward 1981, pp. 33–6; see also DuPlessis and Howell 1982, p. 50). An informative contrast is provided by sixteenth century south and north German cities (Friedrichs 1978, pp. 208–9). The former, which were oriented to the production of textiles for distant apline and transalpine markets, evolved a *Verlagssystem* or putting-out system. The *Verleger* was a knowledgeable export merchant. In the northern Hansa cities where, on the other hand, the craftmasters produced primarily to meet familiar local needs, the putting-out system was much less evident. In eighteenth century England, the putting-out system was less evident among Yorkshire weavers of coarse cloth using local wool supplies, than among weavers of worsteds using long-fiber wools brought in from Lincolnshire,

Lancashire, and Norwich (Millward 1981, p. 34). In this case, as we have seen, the newness of the worsted market was the primary factor encouraging vertical integration. Again, in eighteenth century Bohemia the putting-out system was important in the production of linen, but not so prominent in wool and cotton. This difference was no doubt due to the emergence of an important linen export industry based on the very high quality Bohemian flax (Klíma 1974, pp. 49–51).

The causal relation between the development of new export markets and the emergence of the putting-out system has recently been challenged by DuPlessis and Howell (1982) who rely on evidence for Leiden and Lille. Beginning in 1434 (and into the 1530s), we learn, Leiden emerged as a major consumer of English wool and exporter of heavy woollen cloth. Was this transformation accompanied by the *Verlag* system? DuPlessis and Howell (pp. 49–51) wish to deny that this happened, but their discussion (pp. 57–63) is rather obscure because they implicitly and incorrectly equate putting-out with 'great capitalist entrepreneurs and proletarianized workers', which structure is contrasted with 'small commodity production'. We are told that a few large drapers organized the import of wool and the sale of cloth on regional markets (p. 54) but, strangely, we find no direct statement regarding whether Leiden's numerous artisans owned their wool and cloth. The discussion of Lille (pp. 63–78), which around 1500 developed a significant export trade to various parts of Europe and the Spanish overseas empire in the inexpensive 'new' or 'light drapery', is also obscure.

Nevertheless, the evidence provided by DuPlessis and Howell supports the model they wish to refute. We learn of a guild statute which forbade 'the pre-arranged purchase of thread, which on occasion included putting-out to spinners' (p. 69). Next we read that 'merchants not only had cloth finished and then sent to distant markets' but 'were strategically placed to organize putting-out systems had formal barriers not been erected to ward off this possibility' (p. 69). Then we find that 'the most important enactments date from the 1560s and 1570s. Putting-out arrangements were severely circumscribed first by prohibiting the employment of workers lacking the freedom of the craft and then by entirely proscribing putting-out in the making of *changéants*, which were already coming to form the major part of Lille's output' (p. 70). Finally, we learn in passing that merchants involved in the 'old drapery' trade with Antwerp utilized the putting-out system' (pp. 74–5), while 'others tried, according to persistent allegations, to organize similar arrangements in light textiles, even though such activity was clearly illegal. In 1560, for instance, Lille joined other cities to protest against merchants who placed "concern for their own profit" above "the common good" by hiring rural weavers' (p. 75). In fact, the evidence provided by DuPlessis and Howell serves to confirm the importance of high information transmission costs associated with the introduction of new products and markets in reshaping economic institutions even in the face of stubborn political resistance.

As Freudenberger and Redlich (1964, pp. 377, 379) well note: 'The reality was so complex that no stage model can mirror a *chronological sequence*'. Moreover:

This situation poses problems for the model builder who wishes to be as close as possible to reality. Should he consider the medieval putting-out system as an episode which can be neglected in the model? This would mean upholding the traditional view, i.e. considering the putting-out system as a stage following the independent workshop, as it undoubtedly was in some areas. Or should he consider the medieval putting-out system as a stage preceding the independent workshop and interpret the later one as a relapse? Or must he consider the medieval and early-modern putting-out systems as essentially different institutions?

With respect to the events in the medieval world noted by Freudenberger and Redlich, Carus-Wilson (1952, pp. 381–2; see also chapter 4 of this study) explains that contrary to 'the legend of a medieval world of independent craftsmen', the artisan was 'subject to the entrepreneur at least insofar as he was working for the export industry'. By the 14th cenutry the cloth industry had evidently become more routinized, for foreigners, usually Italians, specialized in wool import and cloth export while the Flemish manufactured cloth or acted as intermediaries between producers and foreign merchants (Carus-Wilson 1952, p. 405; Van Werveke 1954, p. 242).

Thus while stage theories fail, a model taking proper account of the information impactedness problem is capable of following the twists of the real economic world.

At this point in our discussion it is well to remember that the putting-out system appears in other places and times in connection with the introduction of new products for new markets. Two examples should suffice. Due primarily to growing exports of yarn and fabrics, the Japanese cotton industry expanded sharply in the 1890s. This era was also marked by the emergence of large, diversified 'merchant wholesalers' and of a putting-out system for weaving (Ishihara 1971, p. 294). In the period between 1832 until the Civil War, the putting-out system made its appearance in the US in the shoe manufacturing industry centered on Lynn, Massachusetts. It appears that the main employers of outworkers were those producing cheap shoes for the growing southern and western markets rather than those specializing in high quality shoes for the more traditional market (Faler 1981, p. 60). Nineteenth century New England provides us with an even more interesting example with which our discussion can be closed. The early new England toolmakers and armorers produced for the local market in small shops. However, during the course of the 19th century *inside contracting*, a form of vertical integration closely related to the putting-out system, but without geographic dispersion and with greater quality control (see D. Nelson 1975, pp. 36–7), became increasingly common.

Under the system of inside contracting, the management of a firm provided floor space and machinery, supplied raw material and working capital and arranged for the sale of the finished product. The gap between raw material and finished product, however, was filled not by paid employees . . . but by contractors. . . . They hired their own employees, supervised the work process, and received a piece work rate from the company for completed goods. (Buttrick 1953, pp. 205–6)

Buttrick (1952, pp. 205–6) links this change in industrial organization with declining transportation costs and the rise of new markets due to the Civil War and the westward expansion of the population. While the advantages of inside

Putting-Out System and Capitalism

contracting over putting-out are not specified precisely,[2] the direction of this change in organization is, once again, consistent with the information impactedness argument.

NOTES

1. Neo-Marxists, with their remarkable gift for portraying mutually profitable exchanges in a sinister light, naturally speak of how 'artisans sank into permanent dependence on entrepreneurs.'
2. See further chapter 10.

PART III

Competing and Complementary Explanations of Vertical Integration

CHAPTER 9

Vertical Integration as a Defense Against Opportunistic Recontracting

Monteverde and Teece (1982a) observed a positive and statistically significant relationship between the extent of vertical integration for 133 automobile components by General Motors and Ford in 1976 and a surrogate measure of relative engineering investment to develop a component.[1] While Monteverde and Teece take note of the important role played by the 'coordinating properties of hierarchies' in explaining the vertical integration sturucture of Ford and General Motors, their explanation for this positive relationship is in terms of 'the ability of internal organization to reduce the exposure of the automakers to opportunitism from suppliers' (p. 212). More specifically, 'a supplier working in cooperation with the assembler on preproduction development gains a first-mover advantage because of knowledge acquired during development.' Consequently, 'The greater is the applications engineering effort associated with the development of any given automobile component, the higher are the expected appropriable quasi rents and, therefore, the greater is the likelihood of vertical integration of production for that component' (p. 207). If I understand them correctly, the problem of first-mover advantages Moneteverde and Teece are stressing is that the supplier can at the last moment, so to speak, ask for and receive a higher than contracted for price because the assembler would have to bear an inflated cost if he switched to an alternative, inexperienced supplier at short notice.

This argument has merit but it is not entirely satisfying. In the first place, as Williamson (1979, p. 240) admits, the problem is symmetrical: buyer is 'locked into' supplier but so is supplier 'locked into' buyer.[2] The supplier cannot realize the benefits of his specialized investments without maintaining his relationship with the buyer. Moreover, in Monteverde and Teece's example, opportunistic behavior on the part of suppliers of General Motors and Ford would be deterred by the threat of being denied future business. It is difficult to believe that this threat would not be decisive. Second, the assembler might perform the preproduction development and then transfer the acquired technical know-how to an independent component supplier. It is not at all obvious to me why the cost of communication with respect to strictly technical information should be as high as Monteverde and Teece (p. 212) assume. (Would the cost of communicating technical know-how with respect to a component be positively correlated with the level of preproduction development costs for that component?

Third, and perhaps most basically, a variety of standard contractual arrangements far less dramatic (and costly) than vertical integration have in fact been commonly employed to prevent opportunistic recontracting. Thus, for example, in the natural gas industry where opportunistic hazards are presumably great, pipelines are nevertheless usually owned by independent firms, not by producers (see further section 11.1). Exclusive dealing contracts between automobile makers and retailers provide mutual protection against opportunism. This aspect is strengthened by the inclusion of clauses that, for instance, limit required dealer inventories, require refunds to dealers in the event of changes in new model prices, and forbid the cancellation of a franchise without due notice. Note also the mutually protective contractual arrangements between Fisher Body and General Motors (see section 4.1) and the 'second source' options exercised in the automobile and semiconductor industries. Along the same line, the assembler may retain legal ownership of the material results of the preproduction development process, as has been suggested elsewhere by Monteverde and Teece (1982b, p. 328):

The practice of quasi-integration – whereby assemblers own the specialized and dedicated equipment (such as tooling) used by suppliers . . . can be viewed as an adaptive response to anticipated opportunistic behavior. It may very often suffice to protect trading relationships, where full-blown vertical integration would otherwise be necessary.

'Quasi-integration' is in fact widely prevalent not only in the automobile industry, but in plastics and steam turbines as well.

To continue along this line, coal is typically purchased by electric utilities under long-term contract. In the New England fresh fish market the problems associated with small numbers bargaining situations are at least mitigated by resort to a variety of implicit contractual arrangements: 'By far the most common arrangements are those which involve some form of stable bilateral transaction pattern. In its most preferred form, the implicit contract is based upon mutual dependence – the buyer's on a steady supply of fish and the fisherman's on reduced costs of selling – and a system of reciprocation over time which allows the adjustment of the accounts of the agreement upon the arrival of new information about past transactions' (J.A. Wilson, 1980, p. 503). Wilson adds to his description that 'reciprocation . . . allows for the establishment of a trustworthy relationship under circumstances where it would otherwise be difficult.' Another example of contractual solutions to the opportunism problem is that, after the lifting of the Australian iron ore export embargo in 1960, the finance for new mining ventures was obtained largely on the assurance provided by the long-term contracts signed between the Australian mines and Japanese steel producers (Rodrik 1982, p. 540). During the turbulent 1970s, prices and contracted tonnages were frequently recontracted in the light of changing economic conditions. Alston and Higgs (undated, p.5; see also Willman, 1982) remind us quite appropriately that placing great emphasis on the potential for opportunism in market transactions 'depreciates the roles of repetition, competition, and legal remedies in limiting opportunism', while failing to recognise the importance of the 'opportunism that occurs *within* firms, especially *large* firms'.

The force of the above objections is magnified when it is realized that Monteverde and Teece's positive correlation is capable of being explained without reference to opportunistic behavior. The information impaction hypothesis also predicts that the likelihood and extent of vertical integration for a novel intermediate good rises with the level of the required investment which must be undertaken by an uncertain independent supplier. This is a central lesson not only of the Fisher Body and tire fabric examples, but of most of the other case studies reviewed in chapter 4.

Even if the proponents of the opportunistic recontracting – small numbers bargaining hypothesis have overstated its explanatory power, I am convinced that they have told us something important about the onset of vertical integration. This theory also has implications for the subsequent pattern of vertical disintegration. Increases over time in the number of potential trading partners would encourage vertical disintegration, since the victim of opportunistic recontracting might more easliy evade exploitation by switching trading partners (Williamson 1979, p. 260). Note, for example, that in his description of vertical disintegration in Philippine appliance marketing channels, Dannhaeuser (1981) mentions an expanded opportunity for retailers to obtain appliances from various sources (see section 6.3). On the other hand, the accounts of the rise of locally-owned light engineering firms in Malaysia do not mention the entry of additional foreign-owned engineering firms (see section 6.3). The rise of independently-owned gasoline stations and automobile dealerships cannot, I submit, be attributed to upward trends in the numbers of oil companies or automobile assemblers. Cycles of vertical integration and disintegration of spinning and weaving in the textile industry are not linked with ups and downs in firm numbers. The emergence of independent fabricators of copper and, probably, aluminium has no obvious connection to declining concentration among suppliers of these metals or increases in the numbers of metal working firms. (These cases are taken up in section 5.8 and section 12.2.) In these and other historical cases the role of the elimination of small numbers relations, while deserving more research, must be viewed as questionable. Neither does the opportunistic recontracting perspective help us to comprehend differences among firms in vertical integration in a given industry at a given time.

In conclusion, the opportunistic recontracting–small numbers relations hypothesis, like the other explanations of vertical integration and disintegration explored below, possesses explanatory power, but leaves much to be explained by the problem of information impaction. Future empirical research will help to disentangle the effects of alternative theories.

NOTES

1. The latter measure, constructed with the help of a 'source within the industry who is privy to the [actual engineering cost] data,' consists of a '10-point scale, with each component considered to require from "none" to "a lot" of engineering investment' (Monteverde and Teece 1982a pp. 207, 209).
2. Differences in vulnerability to opportunistic recontracting may help to explain asymmetrc choices with regard to vertical integration. For example, oil companies might integrate forward into gasoline because it is historically the major product of refining, but not into a relatively minor product such as synthetic chemicals. For some econometric evidence that may be relevant for this issue, see Lemelin (1982).

CHAPTER 10

Vertical Integration to Control Input Quality

In a large number of cases vertical integraiton may be due to high measurement costs with respect to the quality of intermediate goods. In 1973 Auster and Silver (p. 12) pointed out that: 'In certain cases [contract] enforcement via measurement of the quality and quantity of non-human factors supplied by other firms is quite costly relative to the cost of indirectly controlling the quality of these items by controlling the inputs used to produce them (e.g. when testing a costly item requires its destruction). . . . Our conclusion is that, *ceteris paribus*, the higher the cost of directly controlling the quantity and quality of non-human inputs relative to achieving control via their own inputs, the greater the degree of vertical integration.' Recently the importance of quality control in explaining vertical integration has been strongly stressed by Casson (1982, pp. 15–16).

As noted in section 4.4, the growing demands of the English textile industry for a dyeing material made from India's indigo plant were accompanied by a trend toward merchant control over growing. The quality control problem may have contributed to this change in organization since, as Buchanan (1934, p. 36) explains, not only did the native product become mixed with dirt when the balls were laid out to dry, but certain clays of about the same consistency and color were dug and sold with the indigo. In order to ascertain the proportion of dirt the merchants burned a sample. To take another example, in the first half of the nineteenth century American farmers were strongly tempted to produce their own seeds since, as a contemporary critic observed, 'the farmer cannot be sure that he has good seed unless he raises it for himself or uses that raised in his neighbourhood. . . . Bad or old seed may . . . be bought in the [mistaken] belief that it is good and new, and the seller himself may not know to the contrary' (quoted in Danhof 1969, pp. 155–6). Nevertheless, with the passage of time this difficult problem has been somewhat mitigated by the activities of Agricultural Departments and the emergence of reputable firms specializing in seed production. With the standardization of reels and numbering systems in the Middle Ages, a weaver could more or less guarantee the quality of his yarn without spinning it himself (Jeremy 1971, pp. 355–6). Similarly, backward integration by banana exporters into growing (see section 6.3) might to some extent be due to the fact that rough handling is seldom apparent until the banana ripens. But this problem has apparently been dealt with by contractual arrangements between independent owners and exporters, for example, in Columbia and Central America (May and Plaza 1958, pp. 79, 174). (I say 'apparently', because governmental pressure may be involved.)

The force of this line of argument is also weakened by the ability of the firm to station 'observers' in the supplier's factory. For example, according to Barzel (1982, p. 41), Boeing employs engineers to inspect the airplanes assigned to them while they are being built. Long before the age of flight, in thirteenth century England wool buyers were protected from deception by means of contracts in which the grower granted the merchant the right to name the packer ('preparer') and free entry to the packing operation. This is illustrated by the Pipewell contract of 1290 cited by Donkin (1978, pp. 88–9): 'It is ordained that the merchant's preparer shall be at the costs and the expenses of the abbey . . . and he shall prepare the wool well and faithfully without hindrance from the monks and that the merchant shall have free entry and issue to the preparer while he is occupied.' In the seventeenth century, when anchors could not be made from a single bar of iron, the British Admiralty assigned one of its officers to observe the manufacturing process to be sure that the anchors they purchased were made of wrought iron not brittle cast iron (Flinn 1962, p. 188).

On the other hand, it was probably not feasible to station observers in people's homes and this may well help to explain the advantage of 'handicraft workshops' over putting-out systems (see chapter 8). But note de Roover's (1963, pp. 178–9) suggestion that in the fifteenth century Florentine merchants had the right to go into the homes of weavers to make sure the work was done properly. The emergence of the former system of organization probably relates to the increased or differential use of relatively expensive raw materials. We find, for example, a late eighteenth century Huddersfield cloth merchant who explains that he gathered workers into a centralized location 'principally to prevent embezzlement, as we now manufacture Spanish wool' (quoted in Heaton 1931, p. 52). We find, predictably, that the putting-out system persisted longest into the machine age precisely among those Yorkshire woollen manufacturers who continued to produce cheaper products, where the problem of 'cabbaging' or pilfering by workers of materials entrusted to them was less severe (S.R.H. Jones 1982, p. 136; on pilfering, see de Roover 1963, pp. 172, 178–9, 188–9). Similarly, in late nineteenth century–early twentieth century China, as in eighteenth century Britain, the cloth dyeing process where workers could spoil costly materials was centralized while the earlier stages in the production process were subject to a dispersed outwork system (Feuerwerker 1970, p. 341; C. Wilson 1957, p. 105).

The excess measuring cost argument with respect to controlling input quality casts a good deal of light on the origin and persistence of vertical integration. But unlike the information impaction theory, it casts little light on vertical disintegration (due to declining direct costs of measurement? due to changes in the value of materials?) and vertical integration differences within an industry.

CHAPTER 11

Vertical Integration Induced by Government Policies

11.1 MARKET ECONOMIES

Questions have been raised concerning the continuing vertical integration or joint ownership of oil pipelines by refiners or producers. Klein, Crawford, and Alchian (1978, pp. 310–13) suggest this is due to the problem of 'appropriable specialized quasi rents' – that is, the specialized producing and refining assets are held hostage by an opportunistic pipeline owner or *vice versa* (see further chapter 9 of this study). But this problem has been dealt with successfully in the natural gas industry where pipelines are usually independently-owned. The answer probably lies in another direction: oil pipelines are a risky form of investment whose permissable rate of return is limited by government regulation of tariff rates (Livingston 1979, pp. 324, 328, 335). The Hepburn Act of 1906, which was supported in 1914 by the Supreme Court decision in the Pipe Line Cases, established the status of oil pipeline companies operating in interstate commerce as common carriers subject to regulation by the Interstate Commerce Commission (ICC) which, among other things, was charged with the maintenance of just and reasonable rates. In addition, many states established similar legislation covering intrastate commerce. In 1934 the ICC decided that earnings would not exceed 7 per cent on the ICC valuations of pipeline properties. The data do in fact show that both pipeline earnings and the number of public carriers declined after about 1937. More than half of the latter were replaced by unregulated private (i.e. integrated) pipelines that carried only the products of their owners (McLean and Haigh 1954, pp. 191–4).

For natural gas, on the other hand, the regulation of tariff rates was indirect: the Federal Power Commission (later the Federal Energy Regulatory Commission) regulated wellhead and city gate prices and the implied pipeline tariff. Moreover, the pipeline tariff was not even indirectly regulated when an industrial consumer bought gas directly from the interstate pipeline company. In the 1960s such unregulated sales accounted for a not insubstantial 11–14 per cent of total gas sales. 'Nonjurisdictional contracts' between the pipeline company and the consumer typically included a provision limiting the buyer's use of alternative fuel sources (Cramer 1977, p. 130).

Turning to another doubtful case, the long-lived vertical integration of telephone company and equipment manufacturer, most notably the Bell Telephone System with Western Electric, may reflect nothing more than the carrier's attempt to circumvent regulatory limits on earnings by shifting them to unregulated or less carefully regulated in-house suppliers.[1] As Irwin and McKee (1968, p. 448) explain:

Under public utility regulation carriers are entitled to earn a reasonable return on their investment. A large segment of Bell's rate base consists of plant and equipment purchased from its affiliates. Absent the checks and balances of market rivalry, hardware affiliates, adopting a cost-plus philosophy can merely pass unwarranted manufacturing costs forward to the utility's rate base. The opportunity is certainly attractive.

More generally, as Dayan (1975) has shown, a decreasing cost monopoly can circumvent the attempts of regulators to limit its rate-of-return by integrating backward and transfer pricing the (now) internally supplied inputs above marginal cost. Along the same line, Corden (1974, p. 203) notes that the multinational firm can adjust the transfer prices of imported components so as to shift profits to countries with lower tax rates or reduce the incidence of *ad valorem* tariffs. This will tend to alter the pattern of vertical integration. Again, the depletion allowance encourages integration by making it possible for a refining firm to reduce its tax liability by shifting earnings backward into its crude oil department (Allvine and Patterson 1972, pp. 253–8). Setting internal transfer prices for crude oil above its market value is prohibited by the Internal Revenue Code, but detection is another matter as Levin (1981, p. 219) notes. Similarly, the special income tax preferences associated with resource depletion also provide an incentive to integrate backward into the mineral extraction stage in such industries as steel, copper, aluminium and cement.

The ability to adjust internal transfer prices also provides an incentive for vertical integration when an intermediate good is subject to maximum price regulation. The desire to circumvent problems of non-price rationing, Stigler (1951, pp. 190–1) maintains, provided the rationale for the spate of vertical mergers in the United States during and immediately after the Second World War. (For a more recent discussion of the incentive for vertical integration when markets fail to clear, see Green, 1974).

An especially interesting case of government policy-induced vertical integration (and inefficiency) is provided by the tin can industry. In the early days of the industry it was commonplace for packers to produce their own cans. However, as predicted by our model in chapter 5, the trend was toward disintegration: in 1913, 29.4 per cent of all cans were manufactured by their users, but by the end of the Second World War the figure had fallen to 12 per cent (McKie 1959, pp. 110–11). Many large packers including Libby, McNeill, and Libby and General Foods, gave up self-manufacture. During the 1950s and 1960s many *large* packers including Campbell, Hunts, California Packing, Heinz, Pet Milk, Carnation, Borden, Hawaiian Pineapple, Green Giant, Stokely, Van Camp, Libby, McNeill, and Libby, Sherwin–Williams, Anheuser–Busch, and Texaco entered can manufacturing (Waldman 1978, p. 76). The explanation, I suspect, lies in the 1950 American Can Case in which the courts decreed that 'the major [can producing] firms were prohibited from offering any cumulative volume discounts' to packers (McKie 1955, p. 505). Apparently, the cost-savings from volume were significant for, as we have noted, the large packers in the absence of any very obvious market innovation integrated backward into a relatively unfamiliar technology in order to capture these cost-savings.

11.2 CENTRALLY PLANNED ECONOMIES

The information impaction problems that encourage vertical integration in market economies also operate in command economies. For example, Karcz (1969, p. 254) notes that:

> Efforts are ... being made to promote vertical ... integration of farming, as such, with input-producing and especially processing industries. At least a partial duplication of the conditions prevailing in the so-called 'agro-business' complexes of the West was sought in 1967 by the merger in Czechoslovakia and Hungary of ministries of agriculture with ministries of food processing and some other administrative agencies. The hope is that the reduction in administrative boundaries will reduce the friction between the farming community and the processing industry that led to so much waste in the past... Thus, what is sought is the creation of conditions conducive to the use of new factors of production and more modern production techniques in the farming community.

This point is also well illustrated by the construction in the early 1930s of the Gorky Automobile Plant (GAZ) which was built with substantial technical assistance from the Ford Company. Ford wished to organize the plant on the principle of heavy sub-contracting of parts. The GAZ engineers rejected this approach on the ground that appropriate sub-contracting plants did not exist. In the end, GAZ was in most aspects more vertically integrated than even Ford's River Rouge Plant (Granick 1957, pp. 631–2).[2]

It would appear, however, that vertical integration in the Soviet Union and other communist countries far exceeds the level that might be attributed to the emergence of new economic opportunities. The extreme autarchy observed in the Soviet Union can be seen as a rational microeconomic response to problems of risk, bottlenecks, and quality control. All of these forces are also operative in market economies but they have undergone a quantum leap due to the planning system itself.[3] More specifically, in the model of central planning introduced by Stalin in 1932, each ministry was subdivided into *glavki* (boards) which had to secure basic deliveries for their enterprises by dealing on their behalf with other *glavki* and ministries (Holesovsky 1977, p. 346; Zaleski 1980, pp. 84–91). Not surprisingly, when plans are inconsistent or, as is so often the case, when an enterprise finds it necessary to make changes, it is smothered in red tape and 'finds it not easy to get through the barrier of "sorry, out of the question" ' (Holesovsky 1977, p. 346–7). Given the elevation of information transmission costs, enterprises, *glavki*, and ministries seek to become self-sufficient by means of vertical integration. For example, the chemical industry goes into producing its own transportation equipment, electricity, instruments, and machine tools while the synthetic-fibers industry constructs its own chemical plants.

Information transmission costs escalate in the case of major innovations requiring the cooperation of several complementary enterprises. Erlich (1967, p. 260) cites the hesitancy with respect to diesel locomotives and, later on, the resistance against the shift toward chemicals. The transfer of an innovation from one organization to another involves innumerable meetings of scientific and technical commissions, numbering 50 to 60 persons and sometimes 100, and the testimony of eminent scientists to lend scientific weight (Berliner 1976, p. 103). No wonder, then, that innovators often despair of obtaining the necessary signatures of approval and indulge in the practice of 'universalism'. 'We read', Berliner (1976, p. 102) notes, 'that the engineering design organizations in individual branches "don't know and often are not interested" in what other branches are planning to build in a district. One of the consequences is that each plant is built so as to comprise a "closed cycle" of production, with extensive duplication of steam boiler installations, water supply systems, and so forth.' All this well illustrates what has been called the 'not invented here' syndrome.

Similarly to the case of engineering design, the Soviet Union's machine building plants

have found it expedient to produce a large part of their steel ingot requirements in their own small open-hearth, electric, and Bessemer furnaces. *By producing their own steel, they are better able to meet special demands for steel castings and ingots for their small rolling mills.* They are less liable to be shut down from lack of basic raw steel, a hazard to which supply-oriented socialist economies are particularly prone. . . . Soviet machine building plants all have their own foundries. (Clark 1973, p. 78; italics added)

M.J. Berry (1982, p. 77) finds the most striking difference between the British and American machine tool industries and their Soviet counterparts to be the relatively low level of sub-contracting of components and motors in the latter. Naturally, denunciations of 'empire building' are both rampant and futile.

During China's 'Great Leap Forward' (1958–60) a campaign was launched by the rulers to build ferrous metallurgy facilities, both primitive and modern, at machine building plants. But as Clark (1973, p. 78) explains, this vertical integration drive was not entirely preplanned:

In part it reflected an understandable attempt of machinery manufacturers to assure themselves of a supply of raw material in the face of the low quality and uncertain deliveries from outside suppliers that characterized the Great Leap. Similarly, it reflected the need to secure difficult to obtain supplies in the decentralized plants set up in out-of-the-way places during the Leap.

History has a way of repeating itself. The beginning of the modern iron and steel industry in China dates back to 1890 when the Governor of Hupeh province under the Manchu regime constructed and operated in Central China the Hanyang Iron and Steel Works (Wu 1965, p. 17). During the embryonic phase of the industry, China's machine building plants often smelted their own steel (Clark 1973, p. 79).

Also during the Great Leap Forward many enterprises even acquired farms and food-processing plants in order to feed their employees! (Schurmann 1968, p. 300) After 1960 the advocacy of specialization reappeared but, as Rawski (1980, p. 130) points out, 'the overall degree of vertical integration remains high. . . . Large enterprises in all industries continued to operate a wide range of ancillary facilities, and the frequency with which visitors encounter well-equipped machine shops in smaller enterprises indicates that self-supply continues to occupy an important role in Chinese industrial life.'

The observed pattern is what is to be expected when the state massively intervenes in the economy, forcing up information transmission costs and magnifying the information impaction problem while undermining the incentives of intermediate goods producers to heed the information that finds its way to them.

NOTES

1. Some sort of test will be provided by the AT&T divestiture agreement of January 1982.
2. Along the same lines Baranson (1969, p. 26) has observed that in the 1960s the subsidiaries of United States automobile manufacturers in less developed countries such as Argentina and Brazil are more vertically integrated than the parent firms themselves.
3. As in market economies, the degree of vertical integration is also influenced by tax policies and methods of computing the output of an enterprise (gross or net purchases from other enterprises or of internal transfers of intermediate goods). For the case of China, see Donnithorne (1967, p. 169).

CHAPTER 12

Monopolization as a Motive for Vertical Integration

It is not my purpose in this chapter to summarize and take issue with the ingenious models in which vertical integration is motivated by pricing difficulties for unique inputs related to increasing returns, or by monopolistic considerations including the defense of raw materials sources, elimination of bilateral monopoly, successive monopoly, achievement of price discrimination, heightening of entry barriers, prevention of substitution away from a monopolistically provided input, and the like.[1] I do not doubt the logic or the potential explanatory power of these models. My purpose is to take a new look at some important pieces of evidence in order to determine first, whether they really support a monopolistic type explanation of vertical integration and second, whether they are inconsistent with the information reduction by retransmission hypothesis put forward in the first part of this study.

12.1 THE PORTLAND CEMENT-READY MIX CONCRETE MERGER WAVE

During the late 1950s and early 1960s the portland cement-ready mix concrete industry experienced a merger wave in which a number of cement producers acquired large ready-mix concrete firms. Prior to 1956 only two cement producers had integrated forward, but by 1964 twenty-one additional cement firms entered the concrete market via merger (Waldman 1978, p. 69). The Federal Trade Commission (FTC) ventured a sinister explanation: this merger activity was motivated by a desire to capture customers and, thereby, restrict competition (see McBride 1979, pp. 40–65). Peltzman

(1969, p. 171), however, has challenged the theoretical support of predatory market foreclosure by suggesting that: '(1) predation imposes costs on the predator as well as on the intended victims; (2) if the predator has a cost advantage which can make foreclosure a successful strategy, it can realize this advantage by different means which avoid the self-imposed costs of foreclosure. Therefore, the expectation that predatory market foreclosure is an important goal of vertical merger has a very weak theoretical base.' Kamerschen (1974, p. 151) warns that: 'No firm can make money by selling to itself' and Allen (1971, p. 272) adds that foreclosure is a futile strategy that 'at most . . . will make possible a bookkeeping redistribution of profits without increasing the total' and 'at worst . . . may involve the integrated seller in a business for which it has little or no aptitude.' Peck and McGowan (1967, pp. 530–31) made the telling empirical point that:

The existence of a considerable market for cement sales to other than ready-mix concrete firms (approximately 40 percent of cement shipments) and of geographical markets for cement which are considerably wider than metropolitan areas minimizes the 'foreclosure effects' of vertical acquisition. . . . The presence of [non-integrated] firms . . . implies that barriers to entry in neither market will be raised as a consequence of vertical acquisition and that potential entry will continue to act as a restraint upon the behavior of vertically integrated firms. The existence of consumers who are sensitive to differences in price between cement and ready-mix concrete provides further constraint on the behavior of vertically integrated firms.

Did the 'merger wave' then reflect some sort of irrational bandwagon psychology? I think not.

Around 1960 continuing technological progress and computer control in the cement industry were allowing more efficient use of fuel and labor, thus lowering costs (Allen 1971, p. 261). Correspondingly, the production (short tons) of portland cement increased by 16.4 per cent from 1960 to 1965 as compared to an only 7.2 per cent increase from 1955 to 1960. The cement producers, but not the concrete firms, I submit, saw that these ongoing changes would, in the end, lower the cost of concrete and increase the quantity demanded.

The innovating cement firms found it cheaper to enter a relatively unfamiliar industry by purchasing their customers than to explain to them why they should invest in expanding their facilities. All of this was, of course, over the head of the FTC which, in the best medieval fashion, issued threats and filed complaints against 'foreclosers'. Predictably, the number of mergers dropped precipitously as the innovating cement producers adopted alternative, less efficient methods for encouraging an increase in concrete investment. These indirect leverages included tying arrangements, large interest-free loans, extending credit on cement purchases, and the financing of equipment (Kamerschen 1974, p. 151).

12.1 THE ALUMINUM INDUSTRY

Turning to another much discussed case, beginning at the turn of the century, the Aluminum Company of America (Alcoa) integrated forward into a variety of aluminum products. The explanation for this offered by Carr (1952, p. 121) is quite consistent with our stress on the information impactedness problem. 'Nobody wanted the new metal in the beginning. Instead of contenting itself with making a material nobody wanted, the Pittsburgh Reduction Company and its successor, Alcoa, had to pioneer the way. Oft times it had to engage in manufacturing operations itself when it could not, at first, induce others to go into the business.' Moreover, in addition to the newness of the metal, its technology required the use of specialized equipment.

Not only is joining metal components common to the manufacturing of most end-products, but aluminum cannot be joined by conventional weldings as easily as other metals. Joining is a widespread technical problem among the end-product manufacturers so that one of the principal detriments to the more extensive use of aluminum is the difficulty of joining. Finally, there is a well-established group of manufacturers of welding equipment for use with other metals. Since 1920 some of these companies have supplied specialized welding equipment for use with aluminum. (Peck 1961, p. 188)

However, the 'traditional explanation' linking forward integration with the newness of the metal and the need for specialized investment has been characterized as 'somewhat naive' by Perry (1980, p. 37) who puts forward the more sophisticated alternative hypothesis that price discrimination was the inspiration.

The theoretical argument may be summarized as follows. Given *two* downstream competitive industries with different elasticities of derived demand for an intermediate good, the one with the more inelastic demand will be charged a higher price by an intermediate good monopolist. In the event, however, the ease of resale limits explicit price discrimination. A discriminatory outcome may be approximated by the intermediate good monopolist integrating forward into the industry with the more elastic derived demand. Arbitrage is then prevented by setting a lower internal price than is charged to outsiders, including both the producers in the non-integrated industry and competitors within the integrated industry. Perry (pp. 38–9) goes on to show that when a dominant firm with a fringe of competitive suppliers sells to many downstream industries, profit maximization calls for the formation of distinct sets of integrated and non-integrated industries. The latter describes Alcoa's position. While, until 1930, Alcoa was the sole domestic supplier of primary alumium ingots, it faced non-trivial competition from magnesium, secondary aluminum, and, most importantly, imported aluminum.

Unfortunately, the empirical counterparts of 'dominant firm' and 'competitive fringe' are quite impressionistic. Moreover, Perry (p. 38) himself notes that 'if the competitive fringe supplies a significant quantity of the intermediate product this will operate to limit the opportunity to profit from price discrimination via forward integration.' But Perry fails to demonstrate that transport costs prevented the growth of imports from becoming extensive and thereby deterring Alcoa's alleged discriminatory policy. Relative to other metals aluminum has high value per unit weight which facilitates resale by widening geographic markets (Perry 1980, p. 41). Imports ranged from 20–35 per cent of the United States primary aluminum market from 1909 until the early 1920s and averaged about 10 per cent thereafter.

Perry fails to provide direct evidence that Alcoa actually

discriminated, that is, set a lower internal price for primary alumium than it charged non-integrated firms. The available indirect evidence lends no obvious support to the existence of a vertical price squeeze. In the production of sand castings for the automobile industry, Alcoa's share was less than the combined shares of the next two leading competitors, while in the aluminum cookware industry Alcoa fell into second place after the entrance of Good in 1913 (in 1920 Good's share was 42 per cent while Alcoa's was 25) (Perry 1980, pp. 47–50). Indeed, the total number of aluminum-using firms in the cookware industry rose from 6 in 1906 to a maximum of 38 in 1923–4; thereafter the number declined to 21 in 1927–8 and rose again to 37 in 1931–2 (Hale 1969, p. 440). Further, it is known that Alcoa provided many independent firms with credit and technical advice (Wallace 1937, p. 409).

Perry does seek to demonstrate that, among the five major uses of aluminum prior to 1930, Alcoa integrated more extensively into those with the more elastic derived demands for primary aluminum. He points out that Alcoa never integrated forward into the iron and steel industry which employed aluminum as a reducing agent. 'The derived demand for aluminum by the iron and steel industry', Perry (pp. 46–7) maintains, 'was undoubtedly inelastic: carbon was an inadequate substitute; less than 5 pounds per ton of steel were required; and arc elasticities computed from a market survey conducted during 1942–3 indicate that a price reduction of one-third would not alter aluminum consumption by the steel industry.' This result is consistent with Perry's hypothesis, but is it inconsistent with information impactedness? It is obvious that the superiority of aluminum over carbon could easily and cheaply be explained and demonstrated by one chemist or technical expert to another. Alcoa would certainly not have had to run steel mills to make this point!

Alcoa did produce aluminum electrical cable. Perry (1980, p. 49) claims that this is consistent with his hypothesis since the derived demand was elastic. In fact, Perry presents little or no supporting evidence and, in a footnote, he admits that the 1942–3 survey quoted above produced an arc elasticity of only -0.6. On the other hand, when in 1897 Alcoa introduced electrical cable in the form of simply stranded aluminum wire, it was undoubtedly a new product with an uncertain market. Subsequently, significant innovations took place involving reinforcing the cable with steel. According to Carr (1952, p. 129) wire manufacturers could no more be tempted into cable production than, somewhat earlier, brass and steel manufacturers could be attracted into aluminum sheet. Or, it may be added, than large steel window manufacturers could be convinced to produce primary (i.e. non-storm) aluminum windows (Corey 1956, pp. 36–8). Thus forward integration into cable manufacture seems consistent with information difficulties and fits in questionably with price discrimination.

To continue, according to Perry (p. 49), the derived demand for primary aluminum by the automobile parts industry was elastic. Competition with other metals was close and, in some cases, the parts accounted for a large fraction of manufacturing expense. Moreover, the 1942–3 arc elasticity was -1.5. That Alcoa integrated forward into the production of automobile parts is consistent with both the discrimination and information hypotheses. With respect to the latter we are dealing not only with new products for a new industry, but with a record of continuous innovation. In the 1920s, for example, the development of Alcoa 122 made it possible to substitute aluminum pistons for the traditional cast iron pistons (Perry 1980, p. 50).

Alcoa did not integrate forward into the production of aircraft bodies or casting for parts. According to the 1942–3 survey, the aircraft consumption of aluminum would be unresponsive to a one-third price reduction. Admittedly this failure to integrate forward may be inconsistent with the information impaction hypothesis. But can we really extrapolate from the behavior of the aircraft industry during the Second World War? Perry's (p. 51) other arguments in support of inelastic demand, for example, that 'the importance of government in the demand for primary aluminum by the aircraft industry', are far from conclusive. Further, it should be noted that Alcoa's experimental Job Shop provided special products for the airplane industry just as it pioneered the manufacture of aluminum furniture and the application of aluminum for equipment in the chemical industry. The first propeller-blade forgings were developed in 1922 and later, in the 1930s, came forged aircraft-engine crank cases, forged aircraft-engine fittings and pistons (Carr 1952, pp. 180–4). A more basic extenuating circumstance is the well-known complexity of aircraft technology and the research orientation of the industry. During the 1946–57 period the aircraft industry stood out among end-product manufacturers in inventions in the joining, finishing, and fabrication of aluminum (Peck 1961, pp. 186, 189–95). It would seem that aircraft manufacturers were very much aware of the potential for aluminum. For Alcoa the marginal reduction in information transmission costs from integrating forward into aircraft was probably trivial, while the marginal increase in production cost was inflated by its unfamiliarity with aircraft industry operations.

Alcoa integrated forward into the production of aluminum cookware in 1900–1901. Again we are dealing with an elastic derived demand for a new product. This newness is well illustrated by Alcoa's reliance on college students who spent their summers performing door to door demonstrations (Carr 1952, pp. 114–15). There are indications of difficulties in persuading independent firms to enter production (see Corey 1956, p. 212). Perry does raise a reasonable objection by asking why integration persisted long after aluminum cookware was well established in the market place. In reply, it should be noted in the first place that Alcoa's aluminum furniture operation founded in 1924 was sold to General Fireproofing Company ten years later. 'After ten years and investment of some three million dollars, Alcoa had demonstrated to furniture makers the suitability of aluminum for this purpose' (Carr 1952, p. 181). But the basic point is that the theory developed in chapter 5 predicts that, *ceteris paribus*, vertical integration for a firm will not increase over time, not that it must always decrease. In addition, it is quite apparent and consistent with the theory that today's aluminum producers are less integrated into cookware than was Alcoa in the early years of the century. Another point to be considered is that later entrants to the aluminum industry such as Reynolds (1940) and Kaiser (1945) immediately made far greater use of independent warehousemen than had Alcoa (Peck 1961, pp. 127–8).

This review of the evidence for the aluminum industry cannot conclusively demonstrate the validity of the 'naive', traditional explanation of forward integration by Alcoa based on information impaction problems. In the light of the evidence, however, this line of approach does appear to offer reasonable explanations and certainly does not fare worse than the forward integration to prevent arbitrage hypothesis. It may well be that future research will show that both motives played roles.

12.3 THE PETROLEUM INDUSTRY

Allen (1981, p. 73) adopts the, in my judgement, tenuous assumption that market share stability is the outcome of tacit collusion and seeks (by means of regression analysis) to relate its absence (measured by the standard deviation of the market shares of the major oil companies in each of the states for 1969 through 1974) to measures of vertical integration (the refiner's crude oil self-sufficiency) and size (the company's 1972 national sales rank). He finds that the regression coefficient of vertical integration has the 'expected' negative sign and is statistically significant. However, the symptoms of a high degree of multicollinearity are obvious: (1) the inclusion of vertical integration in the regressions raises r^2 only slightly from 0.3653 to 0.3731; (2) r^2 does not seem to be adjusted for degrees of freedom; (3) when the much more significant size measure is omitted from the regression the coefficient of vertical integration no longer comes close to statistical significance. Allen (p. 88) seeks to make a virtue of the latter difficulty by suggesting that 'statistical inferences about integration that do not consider the effect of absolute size suffer from specification error,' adding that 'this may explain why econometric findings condemning vertical integration as anticompetitive are so few.' He concludes that 'vertical integration clearly increases market share stability.' It seems much clearer that there is no necessary connection between market share stability in states and collusion, that little or no evidence is presented for a relationship between market share stability and vertical integration, and that Allen's regressions have been bedeviled by multicollinearity problems.

Let us conclude on a positive note by citing the results of Kaserman and Rice (1981) and Levin (1981). Kaserman and Rice having failed to observe the predicted difference in the expansion paths of the refineries of integrated and non-integrated firms, conclude (p. 265) that: 'On the basis of this simple test, it appears that the theory of predatory vertical integration [price-cost squeeze on non-integrated producers] . . . is not supported by the evidence exhibited by the firms in the [oil] industry.' Levin's rather robust finding that vertical integration (refining plus crude production) did not increase oil company profits in 1948–57 or 1958–72 casts doubt on the hypothesis that vertical integration serves to augment monopoly power. (See also the discussion of Levin's results in chapter 5 of this study.)

To conclude, I do not doubt that monopolistic considerations play a role in explaining the presence of vertical integration. However, this review of some of the more important evidence should warn us not to overstate the importance of this factor or to understate the importance of efficiency considerations.

NOTES

1. See, for example, Hay and Morris (1979); Kaserman (1978); Needham (1978); Porter and Spence (1977); Schmalensee (1973); Vernon and Graham (1971); Warren-Boulton (1978); Waterson (1982); Westfield (1981).

CHAPTER 13

Market Size Limitations on the Division of Labor and Vertical Integration

13.1 THE ONSET OF VERTICAL INTEGRATION

Adam Smith suggested and George Stigler (1951) demonstrated that 'The Division of Labor is Limited by the Extent of the Market.' One may therefore object to the evidence presented in chapter 4 that for new products with non-trivial economies of scale, the vertical integration effects of information reduction by retransmission will be confounded with those of low levels of final demand. This objection is not without merit, but its importance is easily overestimated. In the absence of economies due either to technical similarities, or complementarities between production stages (economies of scope or sub-additivity of cost functions)[1], *or* information reduction by retransmission, there is no more reason for an *underemployed* X producer to integrate backward or forward than for him to produce good Y – that is, any one of very many entirely different products (conglomerate or unrelated diversification).[2,3] Under these circumstances the onset of vertical integration takes on a decidedly accidental character. If, moreover, there are economies of scope between X and Y production, the underemployed X producer will choose to enter the Y industry; conglomerate diversification will be observed, not vertical diversification.

13.2 HISTORICAL EVIDENCE

It is true, for example, that in seventeenth century England when the copper and brass industries were in their infancy that a single German operated firm, United Societies, carried through all the operations from mining and smelting the copper ore to the production of wool cards for the textile industry, copper and brass wire, and pins, pans and kettles. But it must be noted that while copper is a raw material in the making of brass, the two metals also closely resembled one another in their working – both capital goods and skills were more or less interchangeable (H. Hamilton 1926, pp. 93–5). In the absence of this similarity (an economy of scope) it is at least questionable whether vertical integration would have represented the optimal response of underemployed brass and copper producers. Again, in the early days of the industry an underemployed oil distillation firm could efficiently add the cracking operation because the latter 'was accomplished by merely increasing the temperature and pressure in stills very much like those used for distillation purposes' (McLean and Haigh 1954, p. 10).

Due to 'technological convergence' designers and builders of oil refineries have constructed chemical plants and other process technology facilities; oil companies have diversified into alternate fuels; textile machinery makers have manufactured locomotives and steam engines; sewing machine firms have turned out bicycles and automobiles; nineteenth century dye producing firms have moved into the production of antiseptics since both belonged primarily to the phenol family; and progressive development of refining technology has opened the way for oil companies to produce organic chemicals and engage in chemical processing. DuPont's activities in the area of synthetic fibers gave it the knowledge and skills in heat resistance, elasticity, and abrasives which it later applied in such areas as photographic film and pharmaceuticals. Finally, and most recently, oil companies see an opportunity to produce copper and in this way apply their knowledge of extraction technology.

A firm such as the gunmaker E. Remington & Son added sewing machines and typewriters after the Civil War in the 1870s when the gun business was at a low ebb (Nelson 1975, p. 5). During the interwar period a Hungarian firm, Hofberr-Schrantz Farm Machinery Company, attempted to make up for a shrinking farm machinery market by turning out equipment for the paper and textile industries (Berend and Ranki 1974, p. 141). Motivated by the stagnant character of the sewing machine industry in the middle of the 1950s, White Consolidated Industries expanded into the areas of industrial machinery and consumer appliances (Didrichsen 1972, p. 214). During the depression of the 1930s, 'General Motors (and to a lesser extent other firms in the auto industry) moved into diesels, appliances, tractors, and airplanes', while 'rubber firms developed the possibilities of rubber chemistry to compensate for declining tire sales' (Chandler 1962, p. 275). Underemployed firms often move into areas demanding comparable financial, or managerial, or marketing skills or channels. Thus, in the 1960s, America Brands (formerly American Tobacco) moved into prepackaged foods and alcoholic beverages, while Liggett and Myers chose alcoholic beverages, pet foods, cereals and watch bands. Textron, an underemployed textile producer, has since 1953 acquired manufacturing companies and served them in the role of management consultant (Didrichsen 1972, pp. 216–18). So also plastic product firms have more fully utilized their marketing channels by diversifying into metal products purchased by the same customers. Of course, it is not uncommon to find firms with excess managerial capacity diversifying into technically unrelated products with growth potential.

13.3 VERTICAL DISINTEGRATION

While the Smith–Stigler hypothesis tells us nothing of a systematic nature about the *onset* of vertical integration, it may well have something important to say concerning the *subsequent pattern of vertical disintegration. If* the passage of time sufficiently increased the demand for good X, the producer according to the Smith–Stigler theory would specialize in X in order to take advantage of unexploited economies of scale that are assumed to exist (see also J. Robinson 1934, pp. 339–40). That is, the entrepreneur would shift his managerial input out of secondary activities, including both alternative products and operations upstream and downstream from X.[4,5,6,7] At this point the theoretical apparatus developed in chapter 5 can be utilized. The diversion of the entrepreneur's managerial effort away from up and downstream operations would increase the shirking problem in time 2 and, for this reason, would cause the *MIPC* curve to shift to the left for all operations. This shift in itself would operate to *decrease* the profit-maximizing extent of vertical integration in time 2. Notice that the effects of the Smith–Stigler and information reduction by retransmission theories are complementary in their effects. The former exercises its effect via an upward shift in the *MIPC* curve, while the latter exercises its effect through a downward shift in the *MRITC* curve. It is quite true that the above channels of influence would be difficult to disentangle. But the importance of the Smith–Stigler hypothesis for vertical disintegration is weakened, perhaps gravely, by the phenomenon of learning by doing. As pointed out in chapter 5, the effect of experience with the operations integrated in time 1 is to shift the *MIPC* curve to the right in time 2. That is, the direction of the expected shift is opposite to and therefore tends to negate the one predicted by Smith–Stigler.

13.4 ECONOMETRIC EVIDENCE

In view of the conflicting effects on *MIPC* it is not surprising that Etgar's (1977) formal empirical study using United States data from the 1963 Census of Manufacturing fails to demonstrate that vertical integration decreases with market size. The degree of vertical integration in an industry is measured by its ratio of value added to shipments. Certainly this measure is not without shortcomings but the underlying rationale is sound: the more integrated an industry, the less the importance of interfirm transactions and, consequently, the higher the ratio of value added to shipments. The explanatory variable, market size, is measured by the industry's value of shipments in 1977. Separate regressions were run for each of thirteen three-digit industries. In each case the units of observation were the component four-digit sub-industries. It was found that the regression coefficients of market size had the expected negative sign in only six of the thirteen industries. Moreover, three negative and an equal number of positive regression coefficients achieved statistical significance at the 0.10 level. Obviously, one study of this kind does not settle the question.

Another formal study by Tucker and Wilder (1977) related for 54 firms, the 1973 vertical integration index (ratio of value added to net sales) to a number of variables including: the firm's 1953 vertical integration index; the firm's sales in 1953; the annual rate of growth of the firm's sales over the period; a merger variable (1 if a firm engaged in significant merger activity during the period, 0 if it did not); the 1954 weighted average concentration ratio of the industries in which the firm had substantial sales; the annual percentage rate of change of the concentration ratio over the period; and the age of the firm as measured by the number of years since incorporation. The regression coefficient of the 1953 vertical integration index is positive and dominates the results ($t = 68.55$). As predicted by the Smith–Stigler hypothesis, the coefficients of the sales variables have negative signs in regressions not including the age variable, but statistical significance is achieved only when the dependent variable is an 'adjusted' rather than a 'raw' ratio of value added to sales.[8] A cubic form for the age–vertical integration relationship appears to be consistent with the data. Tucker and Wilder (p. 92) suggest that the latter finding supports Stigler's hypothesis that 'the extent of vertical integration is expected to increase for young and very old firms, and to decrease for mature firms.' Frankly, I am puzzled by this assertion. In the context of Stigler's model, age would only serve as a proxy variable for the size of the firm or industry – that is, for *sales*. Why then did Tucker and Wilder include sales variables in the same regressions with the age variables? Why do they observe the above noted cubic relationship in regressions that have been adjusted for the level and rate of change of sales? Another key problem is whether in regressions adjusted for sales the age of the firm variable really serves as a proxy for the age of good X (the new product). To what extent do the results for firms of 'mature' age offer support to the theory put forward in the present work by indicating that the passage of time ultimately reduces vertical integration even when market size is 'held constant'? Does the initial increase in vertical integration with age support the 'quiet times' argument discussed in chapter 5?

Before carrying these speculations very far, it is well to note that when the 1953 vertical integration index is excluded from the regressions the results shift dramatically: the sign of the annual percentage change in the concentration ratio changes from positive ($t = 1.87$) to negative ($t = -2.40$); the coefficient of the merger variable changes from positive ($t = 1.62$) to negative ($t = -3.29$); the coefficient of the growth rate of sales changes from negative ($t = -6.26$) to positive ($t = 0.36$)! I find these results not sufficiently robust to place reliance upon; the reader must make this judgement for himself. I might add that problems of this kind are not at all uncommon in econometric research.

NOTES

1. See note 1 to chapter 5.
2. The underemployed producer might also rent out his labor services on the market.
3. Similarly, it seems to me that a risk averse X producer seeking to diversify his *ex ante* risk would have no more reason to integrate backward or forward than to produce a different product entirely (see Perry 1982, especially pp. 205–6; see also note 6 below).
4. Compare the discussion of Panzar and Willig (1981, pp. 271–2).
5. Lye and Silbertson (1981, pp. 266–8) considered the 1979 pattern of divestment among 85 United Kingdom industrial and commercial companies finding that 71 per cent of divestment was 'conglomerate', 23 per cent 'horizontal' (same Standard Industrial Classification code), and only 6 per cent were 'vertical' (in the input/output sense).
6. Broadly understood this would include a reduction in the proportion of the producer's labor time rented out on the market (see note 5 to chapter 5).
7. Perry (1982) has shown that, given imperfect capital markets and a negative *ex ante* covariance of rental earnings between two stages of production, a risk averse X producer might diversify forward or backward to diversify his *ex ante* risk. However, it is unlikely, to say the least, that the observed pattern of vertical disintegration can be attributed to a systematic tendency of the

covariance to change from negative to positive with the passage of time.
8. The raw index of vertical integration is the ratio of value added to net sales. The adjusted index equals

$$\frac{\text{Value added} - (\text{Net income} + \text{Income taxes})}{\text{Sales} - (\text{Net income} + \text{Income taxes})}$$

According to Tucker and Wilder (1977, p. 87) 'the adjusted index is a more conceptually sound method of measuring trends in vertical integration since it removes the effect of trends in profitability and taxation.'

Concluding Remarks

At present we find ourselves in the position of choosing, not between empirical approaches of a higher or lower order of rigorousness, but between the latter and non-empirical theorizing and policy. From this modest but realistic perspective I believe it is fair to conclude that the central theory of this essay is consistent with many rather crucial facts of business history. It does seem that: (1) the onset of vertical integration can often be understood in terms of entrepreneurial efforts to reduce information transmission costs associated with the implementation of new ideas; and (2) vertical integration to exploit newly perceived economic opportunities is, on the average, a temporary phenomenon. Further, the information reduction by retransmission perspective provides a comprehensive grasp over several major but disorderly themes in economic history, including the lord–serf relationship, imperialist enclaves, and the putting-out system. Finally, in the confrontation with the available evidence, the theory put forward in this study fares at least as well and probably better than alternative approaches to vertical integration, such as defense against opportunistic recontracting, attempted monopolization, and limitations on market size. Of course, all of these alternatives play a more or less important role in explaining vertical integration.

The constructive critic will not content himself with asserting that one case study can refute another. How easy it is to *say* this. He will immerse himself in the data and provide some counter-illustrations. Hopefully, as with other suggestive beginnings, economists will be provoked to develop a more general theory of vertical integration and, more importantly, to solve the difficult problem of devising appropriate econometric tests.

APPENDIX 1

Marxian Surplus Value, Enforcement, and Entrepreneurship

In order to clarify what will come I begin by listing the interpretations of the Marxian income category 'surplus value' that I have rejected after reviewing the relevant literature. The surplus value of *Karl Marx* cannot be identified as:

1. a present return to the owners of capital goods that were produced by labor in the past;
2. a mere monopsonistic or collusive return to employers — that is, owners of non-human capital goods. This position has been advocated by Engels (1947, pp. 309–10, 401) and by Neo-Marxists such as Maarek (1979, see especially p. 131);
3. a return owing its existence to monopoly in the product market or to the absence of long-run equilibrium in any market;
4. a transfer brought about by illegal activity;
5. a return to superior bargaining skills, superior technical knowledge, or superior motivation;
6. a rent in the sense of a wage earned by a factor of production which, while equal to its marginal product, is greater than the minimum amount necessary to induce it to do its work;
7. a 'rent to institutional advantage' — that is, an employer-appropriated surplus over marginally determined shares of factor inputs which owes its existence to decreasing returns to scale (see note 4).

According to Marx, the employer as employer does not contribute labor to the production process and hence has no marginal product. Nevertheless, he receives an income called surplus value which, since it is not a payment for human effort (labor), is exploitative. Marx tries to establish the reality of exploitation in three steps. First, he strongly and correctly points out that what the worker sells is not labor but his labor-power. 'The capitalist buys labor-power in order to use it, and labor-power in use is labor itself' (1906, p. 197). Next, the labor theory of value is invoked to explain the contractual wage paid for labor-power: 'Like every other commodity . . . the value of the laboring power is determined by the quantity of labor necessary to maintain or produce it' (1909, pp. 39–41). Of course, the 'labor theory' is no more than pseudo-scientific jargon trumped up to give ideological and emotional overtones to the self-evident fact that total product exceeds the total wage bill.[1] Finally, Marx assumes that if *labor-power* is provided with raw land and embodiments of past labor called capital goods (including technical knowledge), it will *without further human effort* transform itself into *labor*. It is quite true that Marx nowhere states this and, indeed, refers to the capitalist as 'taking good care that the work is done in a proper manner' (1906, p. 206). However, my interpretation is supported by the general context of Marx's model and several citations:

The use of . . . laboring power is only limited by the active energies and physical strength of the laborer. (1935, p. 4)

That which on your [the capitalist's] side appears as spontaneous expansion of capital is on mine [the laborer's] extra expenditure of labor-power. (1906, p. 258)

And most importantly:

The general character of the labor-process is evidently not changed by the fact, that the laborer works for the capitalist instead of for himself. (1906, p. 205)

But Marx was mistaken in asserting that the labor-process is not changed by the fact that an individual instead of being

Appendix 1

self-employed works for a 'capitalist' (i.e. is a contractual rather than a residual income recipient). Silver and Auster (1969, p. 278 and reprinted in appendix 2 of this study) recall that:

> It would seem to be a fact of human nature or alternatively a response to the uninteresting and difficult kinds of work that are typically performed, that hired labor . . . will shirk its duties unless the employer takes steps to prevent this. . . . We call these steps enforcement.

It is quite true that Marx was aware of certain aspects of the shirking problem for, in another connection, he noted that 'the less a man is attracted by the nature of the work, and the mode in which it is carried on, and the less, therefore, he enjoys it as something which gives play to his bodily and mental powers, the more close his attention is forced to be' (1906, p. 198). By Volume III of *Capital* (1909, pp. 451–2) he was willing to admit that:

> labor of superintendence necessarily arises in all modes of production which are based on the antagonism between the laborer as a direct producer and the owner of the means of production. To the extent that this antagonism becomes pronounced, the role played by superintendence increases in importance. Hence it reaches its maximum in the slave system. But it is indispensable also under the capitalist mode of production.

However, one strong tendency in Marx's thought remained the refusal to recognize the fact that enforcement by the capitalist is a time consuming productive activity (i.e. labor) for which he earns a 'wage of superintendence'. Instead, Marx asserts (1909, pp. 455–6) that (at least under capitalism) this type of activity cannot be a source of surplus value because it does

> not depend upon the degree of his [the capitalist's] exertions in carrying on . . . exploitation. He can easily shift this burden to the shoulders of a superintendent for moderate pay.

Marx, however, failed to specify the mechanism inducing a hired 'superintendent' to fulfill *his* contract instead of shirking![2] Obviously, the introduction of two types of hired labor-power (production and enforcement) makes the analysis more realistic, but in no way does it resolve the fundamental shirking problem faced by both ancient and modern employers.

If we ignore for the moment the productivity of entrepreneurship – that is, of the time spent in devising the plan of the firm (see Kirzner 1979, p. 188) – the production process can be conceived of as

$$Q = F(E, L_p, K_p, T_p)$$

where Q = output; F is homogeneous of degree 1; E = enforcement; L_p = production workers; K_p = production capital; T_p = production land (as in Silver and Auster 1969, p. 278; reprinted in appendix 2). Alternatively, production labor can be viewed as an intermediate product involving *both* hired labor-power and the enforcement labor time of the capitalist himself.[3] The latter formulation is quite consistent with the newly emerging economic theory of management in which managerial control is treated as an intermediate product (see Beckmann 1977). Given the adding-up property of linear homogeneous production functions[4] and perfect competition in the market for labor-power,[5] it follows that the product attributable to production labor is fully shared between enforcement and labor-power according to their respective marginal productivities. The wage rate (= marginal product) of labor-power is, as Marx maintains, less than the marginal product of the intermediate product production labor but in no way does this imply exploitation. The income category Marx called surplus value is, and must be, the marginal product of enforcement times the enforcement labor contributed by the employer.[6]

Undoubtedly Marx was troubled by the 'interpenetration' of 'surplus value' and 'wages of superintendence' and this probably lies behind such remarks as:

The wage-laborer, like the slave, must have a master who shall put him to work and rule him. And assuming this relation of master and servant to exist, it is quite proper to compel the wage-laborer to produce his own wages and also the wages of superintendence, a compensation for the labor of ruling and superintending him. (1909, p. 454)

The labor of the overseer has to be paid for like that of the worker. If man attributes an independent existence, clothed in a *religious form*, to his relationship to his own nature, to external nature and to other men so that he is dominated by these notions, then he requires *priests* and their *labor*. With the disappearance of the religious form of consciousness and of these relationships, the labor of the priests will likewise cease to enter into the social process of production. (1971, p. 496)

The implication of these remarks is clear upon reflection: even if it exists and even if it is important, the enforcement effort of the employer is viewed by Marx as a 'non-productive activity'. With this we have reached our final destination, for what is really being denied is the productivity of the employer–employee relationship itself – that is, of entrepreneurship. Before pursuing this issue to its conclusion, let us take note of the fact that the employer–employee relationship is *not* required for 'capitalists' to cash in on any presumed 'monopoly' over the 'means of production'. As Camacho and White (1981, p. 410) rightly point out, the latter could be *rented out* to self-employed workers. Under this arrangement the capital input remains the same and so does the labor input, provided that the 'wage' remains constant. Thus the capital goods could be rented out for a sum equal to the (given) value of output minus money wages. Indeed, while the capitalist's money income would be the same as with his own firm, he would no longer have to undertake enforcement labor. In short, he is *better off* renting out his capital. (In fact, the latter 'surplus' would probably be shared so that both workers and capitalists attained a more preferred position.)[7]

The insight or spirit of the entrepreneur could have little, if any, place in an intellectual system which placed everything on an 'economic' footing. Marx, of course, was far too clever explicitly to deny the importance of entrepreneurship; he relied instead on insinuation or what might be termed 'leading arguments'. However, that which Marx wished us to believe has recently been stated by Marglin: 'Rather than providing more output for the inputs, these innovations in work organization were introduced so that the capitalist got himself a larger share of the pie at the expense of the workers' (1976, p. 14).[8] But given the extra organizational costs and the alleged non-productivity of the employer–employee relationship, 'Why didn't', Marglin (p. 21) asks, 'some enterprising and talented fellow organize production to eliminate the capitalist?' (Why it may be asked, would 'organization' be required for Marx's 'petty mode of production'?) Marglin's answer (p. 21) is that 'there was no profit in such a line of endeavor. If the organizer became a producer himself, he would have had to settle for a producer's wage. His co-workers might have subscribed a dinner or a gold-watch in his honor, but it is doubtful that their gratitude would have led them to do much more. To glean rewards from organizing, one had to become a capitalist!' Strangely, not even one artisan stayed in business for himself and realized (accidentally) that he could undersell that 'innovation in work organization' called the employer–employee relationship. Clearly Lincoln was wrong! Truly, it is Marglin's 'answer' that deserves a gold watch for convoluted obfuscation.

In fact, as North (1981, pp. 38–9) points out: 'Since there have been literally thousands of utopian, cooperative, and other organizational forms in American economic history, we would expect that many should survive in competition with the traditional (hierarchical) firm. They haven't. . . . If that evidence were not sufficient, we could equally turn to look at the many experiments in socialist countries.' Sadly, a Nobel prize-winning economist, Kenneth Arrow (1978, p. 477), making 'A Cautious Case for Socialism', seems completely oblivious to the existence of entrepreneurship: 'It certainly seems as obvious as can be that a socialist economy can achieve much closer income equality than a capitalist economy. The category of profit is absent.' How strange it seems to find economists treating economic activity as a zero-sum game.

NOTES

1. For Roemer (1982, p. 95), a Neo-Marxist, 'workers' are exploited because their position would be improved if they were 'to

withdraw with their proportionate share of society's alienable assets, thus eliminating the necessity to trade their "surplus" labor for access to that capital.' This formulation 'has the advantage of capturing the Marxian theory of exploitation without reference to the labor theory of value', Roemer (p. 97) asserts. In fact, however, 'alienable assets' (including people's bodies?) do not belong to 'society' but to their owners, the individual 'coupon-clippers'. Why then, in the *absence* of unpaid labor, would 'workers' have a claim to a 'proportionate share' of other people's assets? (See Silver 1981b.) When Roemer's 'game-theoretic property relations approach' is rigorously substituted for Marxian surplus value, we are left with the profound conclusion that being a recipient of confiscated property improves one's position while the erstwhile owner is left worse off!
2. In sharp contrast J.S. Mill (1937, p. 407) described 'wages of superintendence' as a return to the capitalist for 'exertion' and dealt explicitly with the problem of controlling hired managers.
3. In the limiting case where the marginal utility of work is always negative, no labor is produced from labor-power without at least some minimum enforcement labor.

A 'market syndicalist' might argue that in a cooperative factory, production labor and *information concerning shirking* would be joint products of the same labor-power (see, for example, Schmid 1978, pp. 102–4). This is a conceivable but surely a limiting case. Moreover, this limiting case ignores what might be called the 'punishment part of enforcement'. Even if shirking information were costless within the enterprise, non-shirking workers would have to allocate additional resources to such activities as fining, firing, or even jailing shirkers.
4. Undoubtedly Marx would have mocked the 'professors' employing linear homogeneous production functions, but I doubt that he really would have disavowed this form. Marx may have had something like a Leontief technology in mind for modern industry; fixed coefficients are, of course, linear homogeneous.
5. The competitive element in Marx's thought must not be ignored or underestimated. On this point see Lazonick (1982a).
6. See Silver and Auster (1969); reprinted as appendix 2. Econometric studies frequently assume equality of the wage rate and the marginal product of labor in order to estimate critical parameters of production functions. However, this assumption is untenable even under competitive conditions, since the wage rate must be less than the marginal product of labor.
7. One modern Marxist mathematical economist, Maarek (1979,

p. 114) admits that 'we do not yet know what mechanisms make this appropriation [of surplus value] possible.'
8. Similarly, Joan Robinson (1979, p. 25) asserts: 'By collecting workers in factories and subjecting them to discipline, employers oblige them to work longer and harder than the self-employed would have been willing to do for the same earnings.

APPENDIX 2

Entrepreneurship, Profit, and Limits on Firm Size*

A2.1 INTRODUCTION

There is a substantial literature on the question of the existence of profit and limits on firm size under static conditions. On the one hand, there are economists such as Friedman (1962) and Graaff (1950–51) who would accept the existence of a non-marketable factor of production called 'entrepreneurship', which simultaneously is a source of profits and a limit on firm size in a static world. On the other hand, economists such as Kaldor (1934) and Heady (1953, pp. 536–7), while agreeing on the existence of the factor of production entrepreneurship and its relevance as a limitational factor, would argue that this relevance exists only in a dynamic and uncertain world. Finally, economists such as Weston (1954) would deny altogether the existence of a unique factor of production 'entrepreneurship' and of what Friedman (p. 105) calls 'expected non-contractual costs' as a distinct distributive share and maintain that only windfall profits are legitimate.

This paper represents an attempt to contribute to this as yet unsettled, if currently neglected, controversy by making explicit the role and implications of entrepreneurship as a distinct factor in a static world. From another and perhaps broader point of view, the paper can be regarded as a contribution to the growing literature on divergences of interests within the firm and the costs of dealing with them.

* *Source*: By Morris Silver and Richard Auster. Reprinted with permission from the *Journal of Business of the University of Chicago* (July 1969), pp. 277–81.

A2.2 ENFORCEMENT AND PROFIT

As Friedman (pp. 93–4) points out, there are two 'pure' methods by which an individual can earn income from the resources he owns. First, 'he can enter into a contractual agreement with some other individual whereby the latter agrees to pay a fixed sum per unit for the use of that resource – i.e., he can "rent" the use of the resource to someone else' and in this way become a contractual income recipient. Second, he can organize a firm. This involves utilizing owned and perhaps rented resources and receiving income 'as the difference between the amount he receives from the sale of products and the amount he pays the resources he "hires" – i.e., he can become a residual income recipient.' The individual can be assumed to make this decision on the basis of a comparison of the expected returns corresponding to these alternative courses of action. The question we now turn to is, 'Why should the expected residual income differ from the expected contractual income?'[1]

Differences between expected residual and contractual earnings may in part be due to differences in incentives. It would seem to be a fact of human nature, or alternatively a response to the uninteresting and difficult kinds of work that are typically performed, that hired labor (for the present defined as wage labor) will shirk its duties unless the employer takes steps to prevent this.[2] Along the same lines, steps must also be taken to guard against embezzlement and theft by hired workers.[3] For purposes of brevity, we will call these steps 'enforcement'; these should be understood to include not only watching workers in the performance of their duties, but also ex post measures of performance such as counting, record keeping, plant inspection, and so on.[4] Of course, some of the latter operations would be carried out in the absence of hired labor, but, at the very least, they would be carried out more frequently when it was present.

When our argument does not require a full analysis of the question of which type of enforcement will be utilized in any given case, the following points are certainly relevant: (1) enforcement operations of the ex post type might not, given the nature of the firm's product or method of production, permit the identification of shirkers; (2) even in cases in which they did, the threat of dismissal might not be a strong enough deterrent to eliminate all losses due to the payment of 'unearned' wages and maltreatment of plant and equipment.

More explicitly, the production process is conceived of as

$$Q = F(E, L_p, K_p, T_p), \tag{A2.1}$$

where F is homogeneous of degree 1, and E = enforcement; L_p = production workers; K_p = production capital ; and T_p = production land. Of course, as well as there being alternative types of enforcement (i.e., ex post and watching), there are alternative methods of producing each. For simplicity, let us lump together the two types of enforcement, in which case we write

$$E = G(O_n, L_n, K_n, T_n), \tag{A2.2}$$

where G is homogeneous of degree 1, and O_n = entrepreneur's time spent in enforcement; L_n = non- production labor; K_n = non-production capital; and T_n = non-production land.

Now assume an individual would produce an output of D dollars if he were equipped with certain production resources and told that whatever he produced belonged to him. Next, consider the alternative situation in which the individual is a hired worker – a contractual rather than a residual income recipient. Equations (1) and (2) suggest that he would not produce a product worth D dollars unless his employer provided additional resources for enforcement – that is, in the absence of a need to enforce a contract with oneself, the 'own' marginal product is greater than the hired marginal product. As a result, the individual's earnings would also be smaller, and this excess of residual over contractual income is *profit* – that is, a return which cannot be imputed, for the simple reason that it exists only when the individual is 'self-employed'.

In the above discussion it was assumed (implicitly) that the individual and his employer were equally knowledgeable about production and market conditions. It follows if non-pecuniary factors (racial discrimination, attitudes toward risk and to the giving and taking of orders, etc.) and the 'costs of using the price mechanism'[5] are ignored, the individual would choose to become a residual income recipient. Of course, in the real world, differences in knowledge, tastes, and other factors are often important enough to offset 'enforcement costs' and lead individuals to become contractual income recipients. Thus, nothing in our analysis implies that all individuals would have their own firms.

There are, of course, many ways in which a firm can hire labor. The above analysis seems strongest in the case of wage labor. It is weaker but, in our opinion, still relevant for other hiring systems. One alternative to wage hiring is the 'piecework' system; however, this system is not appropriate for all products and methods of production – that is, in some cases the costs of installing it would be prohibitive. Moreover, even in cases in which piecework is appropriate, the interests of workers and employers would still differ. Enforcement would still be necessary to measure the quality of output and to insure that in their zeal for higher incomes workers did not abuse the firm's plant and equipment.

Another hiring approach would be to offer workers a share of the firm's receipts instead of a wage. However, this system might give rise to externality problems. Each worker might feel that his income would be the same whether he shirked or not. Such attitudes would probably necessitate that employers and/or employees undertake enforcement. Second, the returns to the employer would be maximized if labor input is carried to the point at which its opportunity cost is equal to the value of its marginal product. However, if labor receives p per cent of the output, laborers would carry their input only to the point where the opportunity cost of their time is equal to p times the value of the marginal product of labor. Enforcement provided by the entrepreneur would be needed to guarantee that workers did not gain at his expense by restricting their labor input.[6] Finally, a share system possesses another defect that would probably cause it to be little used even if it solved the incentive problem. Workers typically know much less about production and market conditions than those who hire them, and as a result employers might find that their costs would be lower if they paid a wage and devoted resources to enforcement, than if they offered a share of receipts that was greatly enlarged to compensate workers for their uncertainty bearing.

A2.3 ENFORCEMENT AND LIMITS ON FIRM SIZE

It is easily established that the need for enforcement places a limit on firm size. From equations (A.1) and (A.2) we have

$$Q = H(O_n, L_n, K_n, T_n, L_p, K_p, T_p), \qquad (A2.3)$$

where H is homogeneous of degree 1. At some level of output the entrepreneur would be applying all his available enforcement time.[7] Thus, further increases in output must raise the ratio of the other factors to his own time which must increase average cost and as a consequence introduce a limit on firm size. The fact that the entrepreneur could add to the enforcement time at his disposal by hiring enforcers would not prevent average costs from rising unless the employer faced a perfectly elastic market supply of non-shirking enforcers. Of course, it is precisely the scarcity of such workers and the costs of determining who is a non-shirker that are the source of our entire problem.

It might be suggested that the limit on the entrepreneur's time and the consequent rising average costs can be circumvented by erecting a pyramid of enforcers. That such arguments are incorrect can be seen by assuming the optimum ratio of enforcers to production workers to be $1/n$ and the entrepreneur is using all his available time enforcing his contracts with n production workers. The entrepreneur could double output by hiring n more production workers, the proper amounts of the other production factors, *two* enforcers, and spending some of his available time enforcing his contracts with the hired enforcers. However, in spite of the fact that the newly hired factors are assumed to be of equal quality and hence have the same market prices as the original set of factors (including the entrepreneur's enforcement time), total cost would more than double because of the need for the entrepreneur to spend some of his valuable time to enforce contracts with the two hired enforcers.

A2.4 IMPLICATIONS OF THE ANALYSIS

The preceding arguments have established that the entrepreneur's time is a limitational factor, but it would take a major study – and even that might easily be inconclusive – to ascertain the relative importance of enforcement in explaining variations in firm size.[8] For the present, we must confine ourselves to a listing of some of the testable implications of our model with respect to concentration ratios and some casual empirical tests of these implications.

1. *Ceteris paribus* the higher an industry's cost-minimizing ratio of production labor to output, the sooner average total cost curves will turn upward, and the lower an industry's concentration ratio. Some evidence is provided by the observation that in the United States labor-to-output ratios are typically higher in manufacturing than in mineral industries, while concentration ratios are typically lower in manufacturing.
2. *Ceteris paribus* the higher the optimum ratio of enforcers to production workers in an industry, the sooner its average total cost curve will turn upward, and the lower its concentration ratio. For example, we would expect lower concentration ratios in industries (a) using more valuable factors and/or in which the degree of finish of the product(s) being handled (both intermediate and final) was high; (b) in which a firm's workforce is more spatially dispersed; (c) in which production work is less interesting and/or physically dangerous or uncomfortable. Turning to some evidence: (a) retail trade is less concentrated than manufacturing; (b) agriculture and trucking are among the least concentrated industries; (c) construction work is relatively dangerous and relatively unconcentrated.[9]

A2.5 POSTSCRIPT, 1983

To date the Silver–Auster demonstration that the shirking problem provides a limit on firm size has been overlooked in the literature. Reliance has instead been placed on

Williamson's (1967) argument that a limit on firm size under 'quasi-static' conditions is provided by a 'loss in the quality of the data provided to the peak coordinator and in the quality of the instructions supplied to the operating units made necessary by the expansion [of the firm]' (p. 127). Williamson goes on to say that this alleged 'control loss' will exist 'even if the objectives of the subordinates are perfectly consonant with those of their superiors' (p. 127). Williamson's theory has been strongly challenged by Mirrlees (1976) who doubts that communication losses set a limit to firm size: 'Uncertainty in communication does not necessarily imply increased losses in proportion to the size of the organization' and 'For the firm as a whole, a hierarchical structure does not necessarily impose decreasing returns to scale' (pp. 130–31). One recent contribution by Calvo and Wellisz (1978) takes note of the inadequacy of Williamson's proposition and then seeks to resurrect it by reference to shirking and monitoring. This is puzzling since Williamson assumed such problems away by taking the firm to be a team (i.e. an organization whose members have only common interests) – see Marshak and Radner (1972, p. 1). On the other hand, Calvo and Wellisz do not comment upon (or even cite) the Silver–Auster analysis in which shirking and enforcement play the central role in limiting firm size. Rosen (1982, p. 313) also fails to cite Silver–Auster, although he nevertheless explains determinate firm sizes in terms of the need for monitoring the activities of employees and the 'dis-economies [that] arise from imperfect substitution between a manager's own production of this activity [supervision] and the use of market alternatives, and by limitations on the manager's time'!

NOTES

1. Friedman does not answer the question, but he states that 'such differences . . . will arise, not only as differences arising from market imperfections or momentary disequilibrium, but also as permanent differences consistent with "stable equilibrium" ' (p. 94).
2. According to Alfred Marshall (1948, p. 141), 'It is true even when a man is working for hire he often finds pleasure in his

work; but he generally gets so far tired before it is done that he is glad when the hour of stopping arrives. . . . The unwillingess of anyone already in an occupation to increase his exertions depends, under ordinary circumstances, on fundamental principles of human nature which economists have to accept as ultimate facts.'
3. To obtain an idea of the magnitude of the theft problem in the presence of enforcement, consider that 'white collar employees in the US are stealing about four million dollars in cash and property from the employers each working day' (Jaspar 1960, p. 11).
4. Alchian (1965, p. 34) terms the resulting expenditures 'the costs of enforcing contracts' and points out that they are absent in the owner operated enterprise.
5. Coase (1952) places such costs at the center of his explanation of the existence of contractual income recipients. In our opinion, the advantage of 'central planning' within the firm as compared to the use of the market is that the use of the market would involve many individuals acquiring the same information; this duplication would raise the costs of a given volume of output.
6. For a more complete exposition of these points in the context of share and cash renting in agriculture, see D. Gale Johnson (1952).
7. For simplicity we can think of the entrepreneur's available time as a physical maximum – there are only twenty-four hours in a day. The analysis could be made more sophisticated by deriving the available time from a money income-leisure indifference map (see Graaff (1950–51).
8. In most studies devoted to limits on firm size, the factor we have selected for emphasis is labeled 'routine' and then ignored. However, it is worth noting that limits derived from factors such as external capital rationing and imperfect knowledge of the future on the part of entrepreneurs fit much less readily into the standard treatments of microeconomics than does a limit derived from the need to enforce contracts with hired labor. Williamson (1967, p. 127) argues that a limit on firm size under 'quasi-static' conditions is provided by a 'loss in the quality of the data provided to the peak coordinator and in the quality of the instructions supplied to the operating units made necessary by the expansion [of the firm]'. Williamson goes on to say that this alleged 'control loss' will exist 'even if the objectives of the subordinates are perfectly consonant with those of their superiors'. Our point is that the fundamental source of limits on

Appendix 2

firm size is precisely the divergence of interest between the 'peak coordinator' and his 'subordinates'. Another theory that may fit the standard treatment of microeconomics has been developed by Coase (1952, p. 340). This student suggests that limits on firm size might be due to the fact that 'as a firm gets larger there may be decreasing returns to the entrepreneur function, that is, the costs of organizing additional transactions within the firm may rise. Naturally, a point must be reached where the costs of organizing an extra transaction within the firm are equal to the costs involved in carrying out the transaction in the open market'. Unfortunately, it is not clear to us why the 'costs of organizing transactions within the firm' should rise.

On this point, see also Stigler (1966, pp. 170–71).

9. Marshall (1948, p. 284) lists among the advantanges of the small firm that 'the master's eye is everywhere; there is no shirking by his foremen or workmen' and claims that 'the gain from this source is of very great importance in trades which use the more valuable metals and other expensive materials'. Also, Marshall maintains (p. 290) that one of the problems in establishing large-scale agriculture is the 'difficulty of concentrating a great deal of labour in any one place'.

References

Abernathy, William J. (1978): *The Productivity Dilemma: Roadblock to Innovation in the Automobile Industry*. Baltimore: Johns Hopkins University.

Adams Walter (ed.) (1977): *The Structure of American Industry*, 5th edn. New York: Macmillan.

Adelman, Morris (1955): 'Concept and statistical measurement of vertical integration.' In Universities–National Bureau Committee for Economic Research, *Business Concentration and Public Policy*, Princeton: Princeton University Press for the National Bureau of Economic Research, 281–327.

Adelmann, Gerhard (1969): 'Structural change in the Rhenish linen and cotton trades at the outset of industrialization.' In F. Crouzet (ed.), *Essays in European Economic History, 1789–1914*, New York: St. Martin's, 82–97.

Adler, F. Michael (1970): 'The relationship between the income and price elasticities of demand for United States Exports.' *Review of Economics and Statistics*, August, 313–19.

Aduddell, Robert M. and Cain Louis P. (1973): 'Location and collusion in the meat packing industry.' In Louis P. Cain and Paul J. Uselding (eds), *Business Enterprise and Economic Change*, Kent: Kent State University Press, 85–117.

Aduddell, Robert M. and Cain, Louis P. (1981): 'The consent decree in the meatpacking industry, 1920–1956. *Business History Review*', Autumn, 359–78.

Agmon, Tamir and Hirsch Seev (1979): 'Multinational corporations and the developing economies: potential gains in a world of imperfect markets and uncertainty.' *Oxford Bulletin of Economics and Statistics*, November, 333–44.

Alchian, Armen A. (1965): 'The basis of some recent advances in the theory of the firm.' *Journal of Industrial Economics*, November, 30–46.

Alchian, Armen A. and Demsetz, H. (1972): 'Production, information costs, and economic organization.' *American Economic Review*, December, 777–95.

Allen, Bruce T. (1971): 'Vertical integraiton and market foreclosure: the case of cement and concrete.' *Journal of Law and Economics*, April, 251–74.

Allen, Bruce T. (1981): 'Structure and stability of gasoline markets.' *Journal of Economic Issues*, March, 73–94.

Allen, G.C. and Donnithorne, Audrey G. (1954a): *Western Enterprise in Far Eastern Economic Development: China and Japan*. New York: Macmillan.

Allen, G.C. and Donnithorne, Audrey G. (1954b): *Western Enterprise in Indonesia and Malaya*. London: Allen and Unwin.

Allvine, Fred G. and Patterson, James M. (1972): *Competition Ltd.* Bloomington: Indiana University Press.

Alston, Lee J. and Higgs, Robert (undated): 'Firm versus market: a comment on Williamson's model of the resource coordination problem.' Xerox, forthcoming in *Journal of Economic Behavior and Organization*.

Amsden, Alice H. (1977): 'The division of labour is limited by the type of market: the case of the Taiwanese machine tool industry.' *World Development*, March 217–33.

Arthur, Henry B., Houck, James P. and Beckford, George L. (1968): *Tropical Agribusiness Structures: Bananas*. Boston: Harvard University Graduate School of Business.

Armour, Henry Ogden and Teece, David J. (1978): 'Organizational structure and economic performance: a test of the multidivisional hypothesis.' *Bell Journal of Economics*, Spring, 106–22.

Armour, Henry Ogden and Teece, David J. (1980): 'Vertical integration and technological innovation.' *Review of Economics and Statistics*, August, 470–74.

Arrow, Kenneth J. (1969): 'Classificatory notes on the production and transmission of technological knowledge.' *American Economic Review*, May, 29–35.

Arrow, Kenneth J. (1974): *The Limits of Organization*. New York: Norton.

Arrow, Kenneth J. (1975): 'Vertical integration and communication.' *Bell Journal of Economics*, Spring, 173–83.

Arrow, Kenneth J. (1978): 'A cautious case for socialism.' *Dissent*, Fall, 472–80.

Asia Regional Team for Employment Promotion (ARTEP) (1981): 'The general trading companies of Japan and export-led industrialization.' In Eddy Lee (ed.), *Export-Led Industrialization and Development*, Geneva: ILO, 179–204.

Austen, Ralph (1981): 'Capitalism, class, and African colonial

agriculture: the mating of Marxism and Empiricism.' *Journal of Economic History*, September, 657–63.
Auster, Richard and Silver, Morris (1973): 'Collective goods and collective decision mechanisms.' *Public Choice*, Spring, 1–17.
Auster, Richard and Silver, Morris (1976): 'Comparative statics of the utility maximizing firm.' *Southern Economic Journal*, April, 626–32.
Averitt, Robert T. (1968): *The Dual Economy: The Dynamics of American Industry Structure*. New York: Norton.

Baer, Werner (1979): *The Brazilian Economy: Its Growth and Development*. Columbus, Ohio: Grid.
Bailey, Elizabeth E. and Friedlaender, Ann F. (1982): 'Market structure and multiproduct industries.' *Journal of Economic Literature*, September, 1024–8.
Bain, Joe S. (1966): *International Differences in Industrial Structure: Eight Nations in the 1950s*. New Haven: Yale University Press.
Baranson, Jack (1969): *Automotive Industries in Developing Countries*. Baltimore: Johns Hopkins University Press.
Barkhausen, Max (1974): 'Government control and free enterprise in Western Germany and the Low Countries in the eighteenth century.' In Peter Earle (ed.), *Essays in European Economic History*, London: Oxford University Press, 212–73.
Barzel, Yoram (1982): 'Measurement cost and the organization of markets.' *Journal of Law and Economics*, April, 27–48.
Bauer, P.T. (1954): *West African Trade: A Study of Competition, Oligopoly, and Monopoly in a Changing Economy*. London: Routledge and Kegan Paul.
Baumol, William J. (1968): 'Entrepreneurship in economic theory.' *American Economic Review*, May, 64–71.
Beckford, George L. (1972) *Persistent Poverty: Underdevelopment in Plantation Economies of the Third World*. New York: Oxford University Press.
Beckmann, Martin J. (1977): 'Management production functions and the theory of the firm.' *Journal of Economic Theory*, February, 1–18.
Berend, I.T. and Ranki, G. (1974): *Hungary: A Century of Economic Development*. New York: Barnes and Noble.
Berliner, Joseph S. (1976): *The Innovation Decision in Soviet Industry*. Cambridge, Mass.: M.I.T. Press.
Berry, M.J. (1982): 'Towards an understanding of R & D and innovation in a planned economy.' In Ronald Amann and

Julian Cooper (eds), *Industrial Innovation in a Planned Economy.* New York: Yale University Press, 39–100.

Beveridge, Andrew W. and Oberschall, Anthony (1979): *African Businessmen and Development in Zambia.* Princeton: Princeton University Press.

Bhatt, V.V. (1976): 'Economic development: an analytic-historical approach.' *World Development*, July, 583–92.

Blair, Roger and Kaserman, David L. (1978): 'Uncertainty and the incentive for vertical integration.' *Southern Economic Journal*, July, 266–72.

Bloch, Herbert (1941): 'The Roman brick industry and its relationship to roman architecture.' *Journal of the Society of Architectural Historians*, 1, 3–8.

Blum, Jerome (1961): *Lord and Peasant in Russia: From the Ninth to the Ninteenth Century.* Princeton: Princeton University Press.

Bogue, Allan G. (1963): *From Prairie to Corn Belt: Farming on the Illinois and Iowa Prairies in the Nineteenth Century.* Chicago: University of Chicago Press.

Boston Consulting Group (1972): *Perspectives on Experience*, Boston.

Bowden, W.H. (1965): *Industrial Society in England Towards the End of the Eighteenth Century*, 2nd edn. New York: Barnes and Noble.

Boyle, Stanley E. (1974): 'Why not try competition? A suggestion to achieve competition in the motor vehicle industry in the United States.' *Industrial Organization Review*, 1 and 2, iii–142.

Braun, Rudolf (1967): 'The rise of a rural class of industrial entrepreneurs.' *Journal of World History*, 551–66.

Brenner, Robert (1976): 'Agrarian class structure and economic development in pre-industrial Europe.' *Past and Present*, February, 31–75.

Brimmer, Andrew F. (1955): 'The setting of Entrepreneurship in India.' *Quarterly Journal of Economics*, November, 553–76.

Brooks, R. Charles (1980): 'Structure and performance in the U.S. broiler industry.' In *Farm Structure*, Committee on Agriculture, Nutrition, and Forestry, US Senate, Washington, DC: US Govt. Printing Office, 196–215.

Buchanan, Daniel H. (1934): *The Development of Capitalist Enterprise in India.* New York: Macmillan.

Buchanan, James M. and Di Pierro, Alberto (1980): 'Cognition, choice, and Entrepreneurship.' *Southern Economic Journal*, January, 693–701.

Buckley, Peter J. and Casson, Mark (1976): *The Future of the Multinational Enterprise.* New York: Holmes and Meier.

Buckley, Peter J. and Roberts, Brian R. (1982): *European Direct*

Investment in the U.S.A. Before World War I. New York: St. Martin's.

Burbach, Roger and Flynn, Patricia (1980): *Agribusiness in the Americas.* New York: Monthly Review Press.

Buttrick, John (1952): 'The inside contract system.' *Journal of Economic History*, Summer, 205–21.

Cain, Louis, P. and Uselding, Paul J. (eds) (1973): *Business Enterprise and Economic Change.* Kent: Kent State University Press.

Calvo, Guillermo A. and Wellisz, Stanislaw (1978): 'Supervision, loss of control, and the optimum size of the firm.' *Journal of Political Economy*, October, 943–52.

Camacho, Antonio and White, William D. (1981): 'A note on loss of control and the optimum size of the firm.' *Journal of Political Economy*, April, 407–10.

Canes, Michael E. (1976): 'The vertical integration of oil firms.' In Michael Allingham and M.L. Burstein (eds), *Resource Allocation and Economic Policy*, London: Macmillan, 103–20.

Carlton, Dennis W. (1979): 'Vertical integration in competitive markets under uncertainty.' *Journal of Industrial Economics*, March, 189–209.

Carr, Charles C. (1952): *Alcoa: An American Enterprise.* New York: Holt Rinehart & Winston.

Carus-Wilson, Eleanora (1952): 'The woolen industry.' In M.M. Postan and E.E. Rich (eds). *The Cambridge Economic History of Europe, Vol. II, Trade and Industry in the Middle Ages*, London: Cambridge University Press, 355–428.

Casson, Mark (1979): *Alternatives to the Multinational Enterprise.* New York: Holmes and Meier.

Casson, Mark (1982): *The Entrepreneur: An Economic Theory.* Oxford: Martin Robertson.

Chandler, Alfred D. Jr (1962): *Strategy and Structure: Chapters in the History of Industrial Enterprise*, Cambridge, Mass.: M.I.T. Press.

Chandler, Alfred D. Jr (1977): *The Visible Hand: The Managerial Revolution in American Business*, Cambridge, Mass.: Harvard University Press.

Chandler, Alfred D. Jr (1980): 'The growth of the transnational industrial firm in the United States and the United Kingdom: a comparative analysis.' *Economic History Review*, August, 396–410.

Chandler, Alfred D. Jr (undated): 'Global enterprise: economic and national characteristics – a comparative analysis', Xerox.

Chandler, Alfred D. Jr and Daems, Herman (eds) (1980): *Managerial*

Hierarchies: Comparative Perspectives on the Rise of the Modern Industrial Enterprise. Cambridge, Mass.: Harvard University Press.

Channon, Derek F. (1978): *The Service Industries: Strategy, Structure, and Financial Performance.* London: Macmillan.

Chao, Kang (1983): 'Tenure systems in traditional China.' *Economic Development and Cultural Change.* January, 295–314.

Chapman, Stanley D. (1979): 'British marketing enterprise: the changing roles of merchants, manufacturers, and financiers, 1700–1860.' *Business History Review*, Summer, 205–33.

de Chazeau, Melvin G. and Kahn, Alfred K. (1959): *Integration and Competition in the Petroleum Industry.* New Haven: Yale University Press.

Clark, M. Gardner (1973): *Development of China's Steel Industry and Soviet Technical Aid.* Ithaca: Cornell University School of Industrial and Labor Relations.

Coase, R.H. (1952): 'The nature of the firm.' In *Readings in Price Theory*, Chicago: Irwin for the American Economic Association, 331–51.

Coase, R.H. (1972): 'Industrial organization: a proposal for research.' In Victor R. Fuchs (ed.), *Policy Issues and Research Opportunities in Industrial Organization*, New York: National Bureau of Economic Research, 59–73.

Cochran, Sherman (1980): *Big Business in China: Sino-Foreign Rivalry in the Cigarette Industry.* New York: Oxford University Press.

Cohen, Benjamin I. (1975): *Multinational Firms and Asian Exports.* New Haven: Yale University Press.

Cohn, David L. (1956): *The Life and Times of King Cotton.* New York: Oxford University Press.

Coleman, D.C. (1973): 'Textile growth.' In N.B. Harte and K.G. Ponting (eds), *Textile History and Economic History*, Manchester, England: Manchester University Press, 1–21.

Cook, P. Lesley (ed.) (1958): *Effects of Mergers: Six Studies.* London: Allen & Unwin.

Corden, W.M. (1974): 'The theory of international trade.' In John H. Dunning (ed.), *Economic Analysis of the Multinational Corporation*, New York: Praeger, 184–210.

Corey, E. Raymond (1956): *The Development of Markets for New Materials*, Boston: Harvard University Graduate School of Business Administration.

Cottrell, P.L. (1980): *Industrial Finance, 1830–1914: The Financial Organization of English Manufacturing Industries.* London: Methuen.

Cramer, Curtis A. (1977): 'The nonjurisdictional gas pipeline tariff: a history of competition.' *Industrial Organization Review*, 2 and 3, 130–34.

Crossley, D.W. (1974): 'The English iron industry, 1500–1650: the problem of new techniques.' In Hermann Kellenbenz (ed), *Schwerpunkte der Eisengewinnung und Eisenverarbeitung in Europa 1500–1650*, Cologne: Bahlau Verlag, 17–34.

Crouzet, F., Chaloner, W.H. and Stern, W.M. (eds) (1969): *Essays in European Economic History, 1789–1914*. New York: St. Martin's.

Dahmén, Erik (1970): *Entrepreneurial Activity and the Development of Swedish Industry, 1919–1939*. Homewood, Ill.: Irwin for the American Economic Association, (1950 Swedish).

Danhof, Clarence H. (1969): *Change in Agriculture: The Northern United States, 1820–1870*. Cambridge, Mass.: Harvard University Press.

Dannhaeuser, Norbert (1981): 'Evolution of downward channel integration in the Philippines.' *Economic Development and Cultural Change*, April, 577–95.

Davis, Hiram S., Taylor, George W., Balderston, C. Canby and Bezanson, Anne (1938): *Vertical Integration in the Textile Industry*. Philadelphia: Industrial Research Department, Wharton School of Finance and Commerce, University of Pennsylvania and the Textile Foundation.

Dayan, D. (1975): 'Behavior of the firm under regulatory constraint: a reexamination.' *Industrial Organization Review*, 3, 61–76.

Dean, Warren (1969): *The Industrialization of São Paulo, 1880–1945*. Austin: University of Texas Press for Institute of Latin American Studies.

Devine, T.M. (1976): 'The colonial trades and industrial investment in Scotland, c. 1700–1815.' *Economic History Review*, February, 1–13.

Dhondt, J. (1969): 'The cotton industry at Ghent during the French regime.' In F. Crouzet, W.H. Chaloner and W.M. Stern (eds), *Essays in European Economic History, 1789–1914*, New York: St. Martin's, 15–52.

Didrichsen, Jon (1972): 'The development of diversified and conglomerate firms in the United States, 1920–1970.' *Business History Review*, Summer, 202–19.

Donkin, R.A. (1978): *The Cistercians: Studies in the Geography of Medieval England and Wales*. Toronto: Pontifical Institute of Mediaeval Studies.

Donnithorne, Audrey (1967): *China's Economic System*. New York: Praeger.
Dorwart, Reinhold A. (1958): 'The earliest fire insurance company in Berlin and Brandenburg, 1705–1711.' *Business History Review*, Summer, 192–203.
Dos Santos, Theotonil (1970): 'The structure of dependence.' *American Economic Review*, 231–6.
Dudley, Leonard (1972): 'Learning and productivity change in metal products.' *American Economic Review*, September, 662–9.
Dunning, John H. (1973): 'The determinants of international production.' *Oxford Economic Papers*, November, 289–336.
Dunning, John H. and Pearce, Robert D. (1981): *The World's Largest Industrial Enterprises*. New York: St. Martin's.
DuPlessis, Robert S. and Howell, Martha C. (1982): 'Reconsidering the early modern urban economy: the cases of Leiden and Lille.' *Past and Present*, February, 49–84.

Edwards, Michael M. (1967): *The Growth of the British Cotton Trade, 1780–1815*. Manchester: Manchester University Press.
Edwards, Ronald S. and Townsend, Harry (1961): *Business Enterprise: Its Growth and Organization*. London: Macmillan.
Ellis, Frank (1978): *The Banana Export Activity in Central America, 1947–1976: A Case-Study of Plantation Exports by Vertically Integrated Transnational Corporations*. PhD thesis, University of Sussex.
Engels, Friedrich (1947): *Anti-Duhring*. Moscow: Foreign Languages Publishing House, (translation of the 3rd German edn of 1894).
Erickson, Charlotte (1959): *British Industrialists: Steel and Hosiery, 1850–1950*. London: Cambridge University Press.
Erlich, Alexander (1967): 'Development strategy and planning: the Soviet experience.' In Max F. Millikan (ed.), *National Economic Planning*. New York: National Bureau of Economic Research, 233–72.
Etgar, Michael (1977): 'A test of the Stigler theorem.' *Industrial Organization Review*, 2 and 3, 135–7.
Etgar, Michael (1978): 'The effects of forward vertical integration on service performance of a distributive industry.' *Journal of Industrial Economics*. March, 249–55.
Etgar, Michael and Zusman, Pinhas (1982): 'The marketing intermediary as an information seller: a new approach.' *Journal of Business*, October, 505–15.

Faler, Paul G. (1981): *Mechanics and Manufacturers in the Early Industrial Revolution: Lynn Massachusetts 1780–1860*. Albany: State University of New York Press.

Farnie, D.A. (1979): *The English Cotton Industry and the World Market, 1815–1896*. Oxford: Oxford University Press.

Fenoaltea, Stefano (1975): 'Authority, efficiency, and agricultural organization in medieval England and beyond: a hypothesis.' *Journal of Economic History*, December, 693–718.

Feuerwerker, Albert (1970): 'Handicraft and manufactured cotton textiles in China, 1871–1910.' *Journal of Economic History*, June, 338–78.

Finley, M.I. (1973): *The Ancient Economy*. Berkeley: University of California Press.

Fite, Gilbert C. (1966): *The Farmers' Frontier, 1865–1900*. New York: Holt Rinehart & Winston.

Flaherty, M. Therese (1981): 'Prices versus quantities and vertical financial integration.' *Bell Journal of Economics*, Autumn, 507–25.

Flinn, M.W. (1962): *Men of Iron*. Edinburgh: Edinburgh University Press.

Fogel, R.W. and Engerman, S.L. (1980): 'Explaining the relative efficiency of slave agriculture in the Antebellum South.' *American Economic Review*, September, 672–90.

Frederiksen, Martin W. (1970–71): 'The contribution of archaeology to the agrarian problem in the Gracchan period.' *Dialoghi di Archeologia*, 19, 330–57.

French, A. (1964): *The Growth of the Athenian Economy*. New York: Barnes and Noble.

Freudenberger, Herman and Redlich, Fritz (1964): 'The Industrial Development of Europe: Reality, Symbols, Images.' *Kyklos*, 17, 372–403.

Friedman, Milton (1962): *Price Theory: A Provisional Text*. Chicago: Aldine.

Friedrichs, Christopher R. (1978): 'Capitalism, mobility, and class formation in the early German city.' In Philip Abrams and E.A. Wrigley (eds), *Towns in Societies: Essays in Economic History and Historical Sociology*, London: Cambridge University Press, 187–213.

Von Fritz, Kurt (1943): 'Once more the "Ektemoroi".' *American Journal of Philology*, January, 24–43.

Garnsey, Peter (1980): 'Non-slave labour in the Roman world.' In Peter Garnsey (ed.), *Non-Slave Labour in the Greco-Roman World*,

Cambridge: Cambridge Philological Society, 34–47.
Gates, Paul Wallace (1948): 'Cattle kings in the prairies.' *Mississippi Valley Historical Review*, 35, 379–412.
Gates, Paul Wallace (1960): *The Farmer's Age: Agriculture 1815–1860*. New York: Harper & Row.
Gerschenkron, Alexander (1962): *Economic Backwardness in Historical Perspective*. Cambridge, Mass.: Harvard University Press.
Giannola, Adriano (1982): 'The industrialization, dualism and economic dependence of the Mezzogiorno in the 1970s.' *Review of Economic Conditions in Italy*, February, 67–92.
Gibbs, George Sweet (1950): *The Saco-Lowell Shops: Textile Machinery Building in New England, 1813–1949*. Cambridge, Mass.: Harvard University Press.
Goldberg, Victor P. (1980): 'Relational exchange: economics and complex contracts.' *American Behavioural Scientist*, January/February, 337–52.
Gort, Michael (1969): 'An economic disturbance theory of mergers.' *Quarterly Journal of Economics*, November, 624–42.
Gort, Michael and Klepper, Steven (1982): 'Time paths in the diffusion of product innovations.' *Economic Journal*, September, 630–53.
Goudie, A.W. and Meeks, G. (1982): 'Diversification by merger.' *Economica*, November, 447–59.
Graaff, J. De. V. (1950–51): 'Income effects and the theory of the firm.' *Review of Economic Studies*, 19, 79–86.
Granick, David (1957): 'Organization and technology in Soviet metalworking: some conditioning factors.' *American Economic Review*, May, 631–42.
Granick, David (1967): *Soviet-Metal Fabricating and Economic Development: Practice Versus Policy*. Madison: University of Wisconsin Press.
Green, Jerry R. (1974): 'Vertical integration and assurance of markets.' *Discussion Paper 383*, Harvard Institute of Economic Research, October.
Greenhill, Robert (1977): 'The Brazilian coffee trade.' In D.C.M. Platt (ed.), *Business Imperialism, 1840–1930: An Inquiry Based on British Experience in Latin America*, Oxford: Oxford University Press, 198–230.
Gregory, Frances W. and Neu, Irene D. (1952): 'The American industrial elite in the 1870's: their social origins.' In William Miller (ed.), *Men in Business, Essays in the History of Entrepreneurship*, Cambridge, Mass.: Harvard University Press, 193–211.

Habakkuk, H.J. (1968): *Industrial Organization Since the Industrial Revolution*. Southampton: University of Southampton.

Haber, L.F. (1958): *The Chemical Industry During the Nineteenth Century: A Study of the Economic Aspects of Applied Chemistry in Europe and North America*. London: Oxford University Press.

Hacker, Louis M. (1978): *The World of Andrew Carnegie, 1865–1901*. Philadelphia: Lippincott.

Hale, Rosemary D. (1969): 'Cookware and vertical integration: a rejoinder.' *Journal of Law and Economics*, October, 439–40.

Hale, Rosemary and Hale, H.E. (1962): 'More on mergers.' *Journal of Law and Economics*, October, 119–30.

Halphen, L. (1964): 'Industry and commerce.' In Arthur Tilley (ed.), *Medieval France: A Companion to French Studies*. New York: Hafner.

Hamilton, F.E. Ian (1974): 'A view of spatial behavior, industrial organizations and decision-making.' In F.E. Ian Hamilton (ed,), *Spatial Perspectives on Industrial Organization and Decision-Making*, London: Wiley, 3–43.

Hamilton, Henry (1926): *The English Brass and Copper Industries to 1800*, London: Longman.

Hannah, Leslie (1980): 'Visible and invisible hands in Great Britain.' In Alfred D. Chandler Jr and Herman Daems (eds), *Managerial Hierarchies: Comparative Perspectives on the Rise of the Modern Industrial Enterprise*, Cambridge, Mass.: Harvard University Press, 41–76.

Harman, Alvin J. (1971): *The International Computer Industry: Innovation and Comparative Advantage*. Cambridge, Mass.: Harvard University Press.

Harris, John R. (1973): 'Entrepreneurship and economic development.' In Louis A. Cain and Paul J. Uselding (eds), *Business Enterprise and Economic Change*, Kent: Kent State University Press, 141–72.

Hay, Donald A. and Morris Derek J. (1979): *Industrial Economics: Theory and Evidence*. Oxford: Oxford University Press.

Heady, Earl O. (1953): *Economics of Agricultural Production and Resource Use*. New York: Prentice-Hall.

Heaton, Herbert (1931): 'Benjamin Gott and the industrial revolution in Yorkshire.' *Economic History Review*, January, 45–66.

Hébert, Robert F. and Link, Albert N. (1982): *The Entrepreneur: Mainstream Views and Radical Critiques*. New York: Praeger.

Hennart, Jean-François (1982): *A Theory of Multinational Enterprise*. Ann Arbor: University of Michigan Press.

Herfindahl, Orris C. (1959): *Copper Costs and Prices: 1870–1957.* Baltimore: Johns Hopkins University Press.

Higgs, Robert (1971): 'American inventiveness, 1870–1920.' *Journal of Political Economy,* May/June, 661–7.

Higgs, Robert (1980): 'Urbanization and invention in the process of economic growth.' *Research in Population Economics,* 2, 3–20.

Hill, Hal (1982): 'Vertical inter-firm linkages in LDC's: a note on the Philippines.' *Oxford Bulletin of Economics and Statistics,* August, 261–79.

Hirschman, Albert O. (1977): 'A generalized linkage approach to development with special reference to staples.' In Manning Nash (ed.), *Essays on Economic Development and Cultural Change,* Vol. 25 Supplement to Economic Development and Cultural Change, Chicago: University of Chicago Press, 67–98.

Hirschmeier, Johannes and Yui, Tsunehiko (1975): *The Development of Japanese Business, 1600–1973.* Cambridge, Mass.: Harvard University Press.

Hirshleifer, J. (1973): 'Where are we in the theory of information?' *American Economic Review,* May, 31–9.

Holderness, B.A. (1976): *Pre-Industrial England: Economy and Society from 1500–1750.* London: Dent.

Holesovsky, Vaclav (1977): *Economic Systems: Analysis and Comparison.* New York: McGraw-Hill.

Holloway, Thomas H. (1980): *Immigrants on the Land: Coffee and Society in São Paulo, 1886–1934.* Chapel Hill: University of North Carolina Press.

Hopkins, A.G. (1976): 'Imperial business in Africa. Part II: interpretations.' *Journal of African History,* 17, 267–90.

Hopkins, Keith (1978): *Conquerors and Slaves.* Cambridge: Cambridge University Press.

Hoselitz, Bert F. (1968): 'Entrepreneurship and capital formation in France and Britain since 1700.' In Malcolm E. Falkus (ed.), *Readings in the History of Economic Growth,* London: Oxford University Press, 95–133.

Hughes, Alan and Singh, Ajit (1980): 'Mergers, concentration, and competition in advanced capitalist economies: an international perspective.' In Dennis C. Mueller (ed.), *The Determinants and Effects of Mergers,* Cambridge, Mass.: Oelgeschlager, Gunnt, Hain, 1–25.

Intercollegiate Case Clearinghouse (1975): *Experience and Cost: Some Implications for Manufacturing Policy,* No. 9-376-266, Boston.

Intercollegiate Case Clearinghouse (1976): *Polaroid–Kodak*, No. 9-376-266, Boston.
Irwin, Manley R. and McKee, Robert E. (1968): 'Vertical integration and the communication equipment industry: alternatives for public policy.' *Cornell Law Review*, February, 446–72.
Ishihara, Takemasa (1971): 'The development of contractual marketing systems in the textile industry in Japan.' In Donald N. Thompson (ed.), *Contractual Marketing Systems*, Lexington, Mass.: Heath, 293–312.

Jaspar, Norman (1960): *The Thief in the White Collar*. New York: Lippincott.
Jaynes, Gerald David (1981): 'Production and distribution in agrarian economies.' *Oxford Economic Papers*, July, 346–67.
Jeannin, Pierre (1972): *Merchants of the Sixteenth Century*. New York: Harper & Row.
Jeffreys, James B (1954): *Retail Trading in Britain, 1850–1950*. London: Cambridge University Press.
Jensen, William C. and Meckling, William H. (1979): 'Theory of the firm: managerial behavior, agency costs, and ownership structure.' In Karl Brunner (ed.), *Economics of Social Institutions*, Boston: Martinus Nijhoff, 163–231.
Jeremy, David J. (1971): 'British and American yarn count systems: an historical analysis.' *Business History Review*, Autumn, 336–68.
Jewkes, John (1930): 'Factors in industrial integration.' *Quarterly Journal of Economics*, August, 621–30.
Johnson, Arthur M. (1976): 'Lessons of the Standard Oil divestiture.' In Edward J. Mitchell (ed.), *Vertical Integration in the Oil Industry*, Washington DC: American Enterprise Institute, 191–214.
Johnson, D. Gale (1950): 'Resource allocation under share contracts.' *Journal of Political Economy*, April, 111–23.
Johnson, Keach (1966): 'The Baltimore Company seeks English markets: a study of the Anglo-American iron trade, 1731–1755.' In Stanley Coben and Forest G. Hill (eds), *American Economic History*, New York: Lippincott, 72–92.
Jones, E.L. (ed.) (1967) *Agriculture and Economic Growth in England 1650–1815*. London: Methuen.
Jones, S.R.H. (1982): 'The organization of work: a historical dimension.' *Journal of Economic Behavior and Organization*, June/September, 17–37.

Joskow, Paul L. (1973): 'Cartels, competition, and regulation in the property-liability insurance industry.' *Bell Journal of Economics*, Autumn, 375–427.

Kaldor, N. (1934): 'The equilibrium of the firm.' *Economic Journal*, March, 60–86.

Kamerschen, David R. (1974): 'Predatory pricing, vertical integration and market foreclosure: the case of Ready Mix Concrete in Memphis.' *Industrial Organization Review*, 3, 143–68.

Kamiński, Andrzej (1975): 'Neo-serfdom in Poland-Lithuania.' *Slavic Review*, June, 253–68.

Karcz, Jerzy F. (1969): 'Comparative study of transformation of agriculture in centrally planned economies: the Soviet Union, Eastern Europe and Mainland China.' In Erik Thorbecke (ed.), *The Role of Agriculture in Economic Development*, New York: National Bureau of Economic Research, 237–66.

Kaserman, David L. (1978): 'Theories of vertical integration: implications for antitrust policy.' *Antitrust Bulletin*, Fall, 483–510.

Kaserman, David L. and Rice, Patricia L. (1981): 'A note on predatory vertical integration in the U.S. petroleum industry.' *Journal of Economics and Business*, Spring/Summer, 262–6.

Keller, Morton (1963): *The Life Insurance Enterprise, 1885–1910*. Cambridge, Mass.: Harvard University Press.

Kerridge, Eric (1973): *The Farmers of England*. London: Allen & Unwin.

Kidron, Michael (1965): *Foreign Investments in India*. London: Oxford University Press.

Kihlstrom, Richard E. and Laffont, Jean-Jacques (1979): 'A general equilibrium entrepreneurial theory of firm formation based on risk aversion.' *Journal of Political Economy*, August, 719–48.

Kirkland, Edward C. (1951): *A History of American Economic Life*, 3rd. edn. New York: Appleton-Century-Crofts.

Kirzner, Israel M. (1973): *Competition and Entrepreneurship*. Chicago: University of Chicago Press.

Kirzner, Israel M. (1979): *Perception, Opportunity, and Profit: Studies in the Theory of Entrepreneurship*. Chicago: University of Chicago Press.

Klein, Benjamin, Crawford, Robert G. and Alchian, Armen (1978): 'Vertical integration, appropriable rents, and the competitive contracting process.' *Journal of Law and Economics*, October, 297–320.

Klíma, Arnošt (1974): 'The role of rural domestic industry in Bohemia in the eighteenth century.' *Economic History Review*, February, 48–56.

Klíma, Arnošt (1979): 'Agrarian class structure and economic development in pre-industrial Bohemia.' *Past and Present*, November, 49–67.

Knight, Frank H. (1921): *Risk, Uncertainty, and Profit*. New York: Harper & Row.

Knowles, Dom David (1948): *The Religious Orders of England*. Vol. I. London: Cambridge University Press.

Kocka, Jürgen (1971): 'Family and bureaucracy in German industrial management, 1850–1914: Siemens in comparative perspective.' *Business History Review*, Summer, 133–56.

Kocka, Jürgen (1978): 'Entrepreneurs and managers in German industrialization.' In Peter Mathias and M.M. Postan (eds), *The Cambridge Economic History of Europe, Vol. VII, The Industrial Economies: Capital, Labor and Enterprise, Part I*, Cambridge: Cambridge University Press, 492–589.

Kocka, Jürgen (1980): 'The rise of the modern industrial enterprise in Germany.' In Alfred D. Chandler Jr and Herman Daems (eds) *Managerial Hierarchies: Comparative Perspectives on the Rise of the Modern Industrial Enterprise*, Cambridge, Mass.: Harvard University Press, 77–116.

Krooss, Herman E. and Gilbert, Charles (1972): *American Business History*. Englewood Cliffs, NJ: Prentice-Hall.

Kula, Witold (1976): *An Economic Theory of the Feudal System: Toward a Model of the Polish Economy*. London: New Left Books, (1962 Polish).

Kydd, Jonathan and Christiansen, Robert (1982): 'Structural change in Malawi since independence: consequences of a development strategy based on large-scale agriculture.' *World Development*, May, 355–75.

Lall, Sanjaya (1978): 'The pattern of intra-firm exports by U.S. multinationals.' *Oxford Bulletin of Economics and Statistics*, August, 209–22.

Lall, Sanjaya (1980): 'Vertical inter-firm linkages in LDCs: an empirical study.' *Oxford Bulletin of Economics and Statistics*, August, 203–26.

Landes, David S. (1966): 'Introduction.' In David S. Landes (ed.), *The Rise of Capitalism*, New York: Macmillan, 1–25.

Lane, Frederic Chapin (1934): *Venetian Ships and Shipbuilders of the Renaissance*. Baltimore: Johns Hopkins University Press.

Lazonick, William (1981a): 'Competition, specialization, and industrial decline.' *Journal of Economic History*, March, 31–8.
Lazonick, William (1981b): 'Factor costs and the diffusion of ring spinning in Britain prior to World War I.' *Quarterly Journal of Economics*, February, 89–109.
Lazonick, William (1981c): 'Production relations, labor productivity, and choice of technique: British and U.S. cotton spinning.' *Journal of Economic History*, September, 491–516.
Leff, Nathaniel (1978): 'Industrial organization and entrepreneurship in the developing countries: the economic group.' *Economic Development and Cultural Change*, July, 661–75.
Leibenstein, Harvey (1968): 'Entrepreneurship and development.' *American Economic Review*, May, 72–83.
Lemelin, André (1982): 'Relatedness in the patterns of interindustry diversification.' *Review of Economics and Statistics*, November, 646–57.
Levin, Richard C. (1981): 'Vertical integration and profitability in the oil industry.' *Journal of Economic Behavior and Organization*, September, 215–35.
Lévy, Jean-Phillippe (1967): *The Economic Life of the Ancient World*. Chicago: University of Chicago press.
Lewis, Naptali (1941): 'Solon's agrarian legislation.' *American Journal of Philology*, April, 144–56.
Lim, Linda Y.C. and Fong, Pang Eng (1982): 'Vertical linkages and multinational enterprises in developing countries.' *World Development*, July, 585–95.
Lis, Catherine and Soly, Hugo (1979): *Poverty and Capitalism in Pre-Industrial Europe*. Atlantic Highlands, NJ: Humanities Press.
Littler, Craig (1983): 'Japan and China.' In Stephen Feuchtwang and Athar Hussain (eds), *The Chinese Economic Reforms*, New York: St. Martin's, 121–47.
Livesay, Harold C. and Porter, Patrick G. (1969): 'Vertical integration in American manufacturing, 1899–1948.' *Journal of Economic History*, September, 494–500.
Livingston, S. Morris (1979): 'Oil pipelines: industry structure.' In Edward J. Mitchell (ed.), *Oil Pipelines and Public Policy: Analyses of Proposals for Industry Reform and Reorganization*, Washington DC: American Enterprise Institute, 317–92.
Lockwood, William W. (1954): *The Economic Development of Japan: Growth and Structural Change, 1868–1938*. Princeton: Princeton University Press.
Lye, Stephen and Silbertson, Aubrey (1981): 'Merger activity and

sales of subsidiaries between company groups.' *Oxford Bulletin of Economics and Statistics*, August, 257–72.

Maarek, Gerald (1979): *An Introduction to Karl Marx's Das Kapital: A Study in Formalization*. New York: Oxford University Press, (1975 French).

McAleese, Dermot and McDonald, Donogh (1978): 'Employment growth and the development of linkages in foreign-owned and domestic manufacturing enterprises.' *Oxford Bulletin of Economics and Statistics*, November, 321–39.

McBride, Mark Edward (1979): *The Federal Trade Commission Policy Toward Vertical Merger: The Case of Cement and Concrete*, PhD. thesis, Washington University.

McCarthy, James L. (1964): 'The American copper industry, 1947–1955.' *Yale Economic Essays*, Spring, 65–130.

McGowan, John J. (1971): 'International comparisons of merger activity.' *Journal of Law and Economics*, April, 233–50.

McKie, James W. (1955): 'The decline of monopoly in the metal container industry.' *American Economic Review*, May, 499–508.

McKie, James W. (1959): *Tin Cans and Tin Plate: A Study of Competition in Two Related Markets*. Cambridge, Mass.: Harvard University Press.

McLean, John G. and Haigh, Robert W. (1954): *The Growth of Integrated Oil Companies*. Boston: Graduate School of Business Administration, Harvard University.

McQueen, Matthew (1983): 'Appropriate policies towards multinational hotel corporations in developing countries.' *World Development*, February, 141–52.

Maczak, Anton (1968): 'Export of grain and the problem of distribution of National Income in the years 1550–1650.' *Acta Poloniae Historica*, 18, 75–98.

Maddigan, Ruth J. (1981): 'The measurement of vertical integration.' *Review of Economics and Statistics*, August, 328–35.

Magee, Stephen P. (1981): 'The appropriability theory of the multinational corporation.' *Annals of the American Academy of Political and Social Science*, November, 123–35.

Makkai, László (1975): 'Neo-serfdom: its origin and nature in East Central Europe.' *Slavic Review*, June, 225–38.

Malmgren, H.B. (1961) 'Information, expectations and the theory of the firm.' *Quarterly Journal of Economics*, August, 399–421.

Malowist, Marian (1959): 'The economic and social development of the Baltic countries from the 15th to the 17th centuries.' *Economic History Review*, December, 177–89.

Malowist, Marian (1981): 'Merchant credit and the putting-out system: rural production during the Middle Ages.' *Review*, Spring, 667–81.

Mancke, Richard B. (1972): 'Iron ore and steel: a case study of the economic causes and consequences of vertical integration.' *Journal of Industrial Economics*, July, 220–29.

Marglin, Stephen A. (1976): 'What do bosses do? The origins and functions of hierarchy in capitalist production.' In André Gorz (ed.), *The Division of Labor: The Labor Process and Class Struggle in Modern Capitalism*, Atlantic Highlands, NJ: Humanities Press, 13–54.

Markham, Jesse W. (1950): 'Integration in the textile industry.' *Harvard Business Review*, January, 74–88.

Marshak, Jacob and Radner, Roy (1972): *Economic Theory of Teams*. New Haven: Yale University Press.

Marshall, Alfred (1948): *Principles of Economics*. 8th edn. New York: Macmillan.

Martin, David Dale (1977): 'The computer industry.' In Walter Adams (ed.), *The Structure of American Industry*, 5th edn., New York: Macmillan, 285–311.

Martin, J. Rod (1979): 'Beef.' In Lyle P. Schertz et al., *Another Revolution in U.S. Farming?*, Washington DC: US Dept. of Agriculture, 85–118.

Marx, Karl (1906): *Capital*, Vol. I. New York: Modern Library.

Marx, Karl (1909): *Capital*, Vol. II. Chicago: Kerr.

Marx, Karl (1935): *Value, Price, and Profit*. New York: International Publishers.

Marx, Karl (1971): *Theories of Surplus Value*, Vol. IV of *Capital*, Part III. Moscow: Progress Publishers.

Mathias, Peter (1967): *Retailing Revolution: A History of Multiple Retailing in the Food Trades Based Upon the Allied Suppliers of Companies*. London: Longmans.

Mathias, Peter (1975): 'Conflicts of function in the rise of big business: the British experience.' In Harold F. Williamson (ed.), *Evolution of International Management Structures*, Newark: University of Delaware Press, 40–58.

Maxcy, G. (1958): 'The motor industry.' In Lesley P. Cook (ed.), *Effects of Mergers: Six Studies*, London: Allen & Unwin, 351–93.

May, Stacy and Plaza, Galo (1958): *The United Fruit Company in Latin America*. Washington DC: National Planning Association.

Mayhew, Alan (1973): *Rural Settlement and Farming in Germany*. New York: Barnes and Noble.

Mighell, Ronald L. and Jones, Lawrence A. (1963): 'Vertical

coordination in agriculture.' *Agricultural Economic Report* No. 19, US Department of Agriculture, Economic Research Service, Farm Economics Division, Washington DC, February.
Mill, John Stuart (1937): *Principles of Political Economy*. London: Longmans, Green.
Miller, Edward and Hatcher, John (1978): *Medieval England – Rural Society and Economic Change, 1086–1349*, London: Longmans.
Millward, R. (1981): 'The emergence of wage labor in early modern England.' *Explorations in Economic History*, January, 21–39.
Millward, R. (1982): 'An economic analysis of the organization of serfdom in Eastern Europe.' *Journal of Economic History*, September, 513–48.
Mirrlees, James A. (1976): 'The optimal structure of incentives and authority.' *Bell Journal of Economics*, Spring, 105–31.
Mitchell, Edward J. (ed.) (1976): *Vertical Integration in the Oil Industry*. Washington DC: American Enterprise Institute.
Monteverde, Kirk and Teece, David J. (1982a): 'Supplier switching costs and vertical integration in the automobile industry.' *Bell Journal of Economics*, Spring, 206–13.
Monteverde, Kirk and Teece, David J. (1982b): 'Appropriable rents and quasi-vertical integration.' *Journal of Law and Economics*, October, 321–8.
Moran, Theodore H. (1974): *Multinational Corporations and the Politics of Dependence: Copper in Chile*. Princeton: Princeton University Press.
Mueller, Dennis C. (1976): 'Information, mobility, and profit.' *Kyklos*, 29, 419–48.
Mueller, Willard F. and Collins, Norman (1957): 'Grower-processor integration in fruit and vegetable marketing.' *Journal of Farm Economics*, December, 1471–83.
Myrdal, Gunnar (1957): *Economic Theory and Under-Developed Regions*. London: Duckworth.

Nafziger, E. Wayne (1978): *Class, Caste, and Entrepreneurship: A Study of Indian Industrialists*. Honolulu: University of Hawaii Press for East-West Center.
Navin, Thomas R. (1951): 'Innovation and management policies, the textile industry: influence of the market on management.' *Bulletin of the Business Historical Society*, March, 15–30.
Needham, Douglas (1978): *The Economics of Industrial Structure: Conduct and Performance*. New York: St. Martin's.
Nelson, Daniel (1975): *Managers and Workers, Origin of the New Factory*

System in the United States, 1880–1920. Madison: University of Wisconsin Press.
Nelson, Ralph L. (1959): *Merger Movements in American Industry, 1895–1956.* Princeton: Princeton University Press for the National Bureau of Economic Research.
Nelson, Richard R. and Winter, Sidney (1982): *An Evolutionary Theory of Economic Change.* Cambridge, Mass.: Harvard University Press.
Newbury, Colin W. (1969): 'Trade and authority in West Africa from 1850 to 1880.' In L.H. Gann and Peter Duignan (eds), *Colonialism in Africa: Vol. I, The History and Politics of Colonialism, 1870–1914,* London: Cambridge University Press, 66–99.
Nichtweiss, Johannes (1979): 'The second serfdom and the so-called "Prussian way".' *Review,* Summer, 99–140.
North, Douglass C. (1981): *Structure and Change in Economic History.* New York: Norton.

Oliver, Henry Edmund (1907): *Roman Economic Conditions to the Close of the Republic.* Toronto: University of Toronto Press, (reprinted 1966).

Panzar, John C. and Willig, Robert D. (1981): 'Economies of scope.' *American Economic Review,* May, 268–72.
Papanek, Gustav F. (1962): 'The development of entrepreneurship.' *American Economic Review,* May, 46–58.
Papanek, Gustav F. (1967): *Pakistan's Development: Social Goals and Private Incentives.* Cambridge, Mass.: Harvard University Press.
Parker, J.E.S. (1974): *The Economics of Innovation: The National and Multinational Enterprise in Technological Change.* London: Longmans.
Passer, Harold C. (1953): *The Electrical Manufacturers, 1875–1900: A Study in Competition, Entrepreneurship, Technical Change, and Economic Growth.* Cambridge, Mass.: Harvard University Press.
Pavlovsky, George (1930): *Agricultural Russia on the Eve of the Revolution.* New York: Fertig, (reprinted 1968).
Peck, Merton J. (1961): *Competition in the Aluminum Industry, 1944–1958.* Cambridge, Mass.: Harvard University Press.
Peck, Merton J. and McGowan, John J. (1967): 'Vertical integration in cement: a critical examination of the FTC staff report.' *Antitrust Bulletin,* Summer, 505–31.
Peltzman, Sam (1969): 'Issues in vertical integration policy.' In J. Fred Weston and Sam Peltzman (eds), *Public Policy Towards*

Mergers, Pacific Palisades, California: Goodyear, 167–76.
Penrose, Edith Tilton (1959): *The Theory of the Growth of the Firm*. Oxford: Basil Blackwell.
Perkins, Edwin J. (1980): *The Economy of Colonial America*. New York: Columbia University Press.
Perkins, J.A. (1981): 'The agricultural revolution in Germany, 1850–1914.' *Journal of European Economic History*, Spring, 71–118.
Perry, Martin K. (1980): 'Forward integration by Alcoa: 1888–1930.' *Journal of Industrial Economics*, September, 37–53.
Perry, Martin K. (1982): 'Vertical integration by competitive firms: uncertainty and diversification.' *Southern Economic Journal*, July, 201–08.
Petit, Paul (1976): *Pax Romana*. Berkeley: University of California Press.
Phillips, W.G. (1956): *The Agricultural Implement Industry in Canada*. Toronto: University of Toronto Press.
Porter, Glenn and Livesay, Harold C. (1971): *Merchants and Manufacturing: Studies in the Changing Structure of Nineteenth Century Marketing*. Baltimore: Johns Hopkins University Press.
Porter, M.E. and Spence, A.M. (1977): 'Vertical integration and differentiated inputs.' *Discussion Paper* 576, Harvard Institute of Economic Research, September.
Postan, M.M. (1973): 'Economic relations between Eastern and Western Europe.' In M.M. Postan, *Medieval Trade and Finance*, London: Cambridge University Press, 305–34.
Potter, T.W. (1979): *The Changing Landscape of South Etruria*. New York: St. Martin's.
Prescott, Edward C. and Visscher, Michael (1980): 'Organization capital.' *Journal of Political Economy*, June, 446–61.

Rae, John B. (1959): *American Automobile Manufacturers: The First Forty Years*. Philadelphia: Chilton.
Rae, John B. (1982): *Nissan/Datsun: A History of Nissan Motor Corporation in the U.S.A., 1960–1980*. New York: McGraw–Hill.
Rathbone, D.W. (1981): 'The development of agriculture in the "Ager Cosanus" during the Roman Republic: problems of evidence and interpretation.' *Journal of Roman Studies*, LXXI, 10–23.
Ravenscraft, David J. (1983): 'Structure–profit relationships at the line of business and industry level.' *Review of Economics and Statistics*, February, 22–31.
Rawski, Thomas G. (1980): *China's Transition to Industrialism: Producer*

Goods and Economic Development in the Twentieth Century. Ann Arbor: University of Michigan Press.

Richardson, G.B. (1960): *Information and Investment: A Study in the Working of the Competitive Economy.* London: Oxford University Press.

Robert, Joseph C. (1952): *The Story of Tobacco in America.* New York: Knopf.

Robinson, E.A.G. (1935): *The Structure of Competitive Industry.* New York: Pitman.

Robinson, Joan (1954): *The Economics of Imperfect Competition.* London: Macmillan.

Robinson, Joan (1979): *Aspects of Development and Underdevelopment.* Cambridge: Cambridge University Press.

Rodrik, Dani (1982): 'Managing resource dependency: the United States and Japan in the markets for copper, iron ore and bauxite.' *World Development,* July, 541–60.

Roemer, John E. (1982): 'Exploitation, alternatives and socialism.' *Economic Journal,* March, 87–107.

Ronen, Joshua (ed.) (1983): *Entrepreneurship.* Lexington, Mass.: Lexington Books for Price Institute of Entrepreneurial Studies.

de Roover, Raymond (1963): *The Rise and Decline of the Medici Bank, 1397–1494.* New York: Norton.

de Roover, Raymond (1974): *Business, Banking, and Economic Thought in Late Medieval and Early Modern Europe.* Chicago: University of Chicago Press.

Rosen, Sherwin (1972): 'Learning by experience as a joint product.' *Quarterly Journal of Economics,* August, 366–82.

Rosen, Sherwin (1982): 'Authority, control, and the distribution of earnings.' *Bell Journal of Economics,* Autumn, 311–23.

Rosenberg, Nathan (1963): 'Technological change in the machine tool industry, 1840–1910.' *Journal of Economic History,* December, 414–43.

Roy, Ewell Paul (1963): *Contract Farming, U.S.A.* Danville, Ill.: Interstate.

Rubin, Paul H. (1973): 'The expansion of firms.' *Journal of Political Economy,* July/August, 936–49.

Safford, Frank R. (1982): 'Modes of production and planter hegemony in two coffee economies: a review.' *Agricultural History,* April, 453–62.

Saham, Junid (1980): *British Industrial Investment in Malaysia, 1963–1971.* Oxford: Oxford University Press.

Samuelson, Paul A. (1971): 'Understanding the Marxian notion of exploitation: a summary of the so-called transformation problem between Marxian values and competitive prices.' *Journal of Economic Literature*, June, 399–431.

Schaeffer, Donald and Schmitz, Mark (1982): 'Efficiency in Antebellum southern agriculture: a covariance approach.' *Southern Economic Journal*, July 88–98.

Schmalensee, Richard (1973): 'A note on the theory of vertical integration.' *Journal of Political Economy*, March/April, 442–9.

Schmid, A. Allan (1978): *Property, Power, and Public Choice*. New York: Praeger.

Schmitt, Hans A. (1975): 'Landed and moneyed princes: the harvest of traditional conflict in German business and politics.' In Harold F. Williamson (ed.), *Evolution of International Management Structures*. Newark: University of Delaware Press, 67–88.

Schrader, Lee F. (1980): 'Farm structure: eggs.' In *Farm Structure*, Committee on Agriculture, Nutrition, and Forestry, US Senate, Washington DC: US Government Printing Office, 216–26.

Schumpeter, Joseph A. (1934): *The Theory of Economic Development: An Inquiry Into Profits, Capital, Credit, Interest, and the Business Cycle*. Cambridge, Mass.: Harvard University Press.

Schurmann, Franz (1968): *Ideology and Organization in Communist China*, 2nd. edn. Berkeley: University of California Press.

Seagraves, J.A. and Bishop, C.E. (1958): 'Impacts of vertical integration on output, price, and industry structure.' *Journal of Farm Economics*, December, 1814–21.

Semple, Ellen Churchill (1931): *The Geography of the Mediterranean Region: Its Relation to Ancient History*. New York: Holt.

Silver, Morris (1977): 'Economic theory of the constitutional separation of powers.' *Public Choice*, Spring, 95–107.

Silver, Morris (1981a): 'Adaptations to information impactedness: a survey.' In Malcolm Galatin and Robert Leiter (eds), *Economics of Information*, Boston: Martinus Nijhoff, 104–18.

Silver, Morris (1981b): 'Men, monkeys, and morals: a property rights theory of social justice.' In Randolph L. Braham (ed.), *Social Justice*, Boston: Martinus Nijhoff, 121–44.

Silver, Morris (1983): *Prophets and Markets: The Political Economy of Ancient Israel*. Boston: Kluwer-Nijhoff.

Silver, Morris and Auster, Richard (1969): 'Entrepreneurship, profit, and limits on firm size.' *Journal of Business*, July, 277–81. Reprinted as Appendix 2.

Simon, Herbert A. (1957): 'A formal theory of the employment relation.' In Herbert A. Simon (ed.), *Models of Man*, New York: Wiley, 183–95.

Simon, Herbert A. (1972): 'Theories of bounded rationality.' In C.B. McGuire and Roy Radner (eds), *Decision and Organization*, Amsterdam: North Holland, 161–76.

Spence, A. Michael (1981): 'The learning curve and competition.' *Bell Journal of Economics*, Spring, 49–70.

Spruill, Charles R. (1982): *Conglomerates and the Evolution of Capitalism*. Carbondale: Southern Illinois University Press.

Starr, Chester G. (1977): *The Economic and Social Growth of Early Greece, 800–500 BC*. New York: Oxford University Press.

Stein, Stanley J. (1957): *The Brazilian Cotton Manufacture: Textile Enterprise in an Underdeveloped Area*. Cambridge, Mass.: Harvard University Press.

Stigler, George J. (1951): 'The division of labor is limited by the extent of the market.' *Journal of Political Economy*, June, 183–93.

Stigler, George J. (1966): *The Theory of Price*, 3rd edn. New York: Macmillan.

Strassman, W. Paul (1959): *Risk and Technological Innovation: American Manufacturing Methods During the Nineteenth Century*. Ithaca: Cornell University Press.

Tamura, Masonori (1971): 'The evolution of various forms of contractual marketing systems in Japan.' In Donald N. Thompson (ed.), *Contractual Marketing Systems*, Lexington, Mass.: Heath, 271–92.

Teece, David J. (1976): 'Vertical integration in the U.S. oil industry.' In Edward J. Mitchell (ed.), *Vertical Integration in the Oil Industry*, Washington DC: American Enterprise Institute, 105–89.

Teece, David J. (1980): 'Economies of scope and the scope of the enterprise.' *Journal of Economic Behavior and Organization*, 1, 223–47.

Thirsk, Joan (1978): *Economic Policy and Projects: The Development of a Consumer Society in Early Modern England*. Oxford: Oxford University Press.

Thoburn, J.T. (1973): 'Exports and the Malaysian engineering industry: a case study of backward linkage.' *Oxford Bulletin of Economics and Statistics*, May, 91–117.

Thoburn, J.T. (1977): *Primary Commodity Exports and Economic Development: Theory, Evidence and a Study of Malaysia*. New York: Wiley.

Thompson, Donald N. (ed.) (1971): *Contractual Marketing Systems.* Lexington, Mass.: Heath.

Tilly, Richard (1982): 'Mergers, external growth, and finance in the development of large-scale enterprise in Germany, 1880–1913.' *Journal of History,* September, 629–58.

Tipton, Frank B. Jr (1976): *Regional Variations in the Economic Development of Germany During the Nineteenth Century.* Middletown, Conn.: Wesleyan University Press.

Topolski, Jerzy (1981): 'Continuity and discontinuity in the development of the feudal system in Eastern Europe (Xth to XVIIth centuries).' *Journal of European Economic History,* Fall, 373–400.

Tucker, Irwin B. and Wilder, Ronald P. (1977): 'Trends in vertical integration in the U.S. manufacturing sector.' *Journal of Industrial Economics,* September, 81–94.

Unger, Richard W. (1978): *Dutch Shipbuilding Before 1800: Ships and Guilds.* Assen/Amsterdam: Van Gorcum.

Vernon, John M. and Graham, Daniel A. (1971): 'Profitability of monopolization by vertical integration.' *Journal of Political Economy,* July/August, 924–5.

Vernon, Raymond (1966): 'International investment and international trade in the product cycle.' *Quarterly Journal of Economics,* May, 190–207.

De Vries, Jan (1976): *Economy of Europe in an Age of Crisis.* London: Cambridge University Press.

Waldman, Don E. (1978): *Antitrust Action and Market Structure.* Lexington, Mass.: Heath.

Wallace, Donald H. (1937): *Market Control in the Aluminum Industry.* Cambridge, Mass.: Harvard University Press.

Walsh, Margaret (1982): 'From pork merchant to meat packer: the midwestern meat industry in the mid nineteenth century.' *Agricultural History,* January, 127–37.

Ware, Caroline F. (1931): *The Early New England Cotton Manufacture: A Study in Industrial Beginnings.* Boston: Houghton Mifflin.

Warren-Boulton, Frederick (1978): *Vertical Control of Markets: Business and Labor Practices.* Cambridge, Mass.: Ballinger.

Waswo, Ann (1977): *Japanese Landlords: The Decline of a Rural Elite.* Berkeley: University of California Press.

Waterson, Michael (1982): 'Vertical integration, variable proportions and oligopoly.' *Economic Journal,* March, 129–44.

Wells, Donald A. (1971): 'Aramco: the evolution of an oil concession.' In Raymond F. Mikesell (ed.), *Foreign Investment in the Petroleum and Mineral Industries*, Baltimore: Johns Hopkins University Press for Resources for the Future, 216–36.

Van Werveke, H. (1954): 'Industrial growth in the Middle Ages: the cloth industry in Flanders.' *Economic History Review*, April, 237–45.

Westfield, Fred M. (1981): 'Vertical integration: does product price rise or fall?' *American Economic Review*, June, 334–46.

Weston, J. Fred. (1954): 'The profit concept: a restatement.' *Journal of Political Economy*, April, 152–70.

White, K.D. (1970): *Roman Farming*, Ithaca: Cornell University Press.

Wilkins, Mira (1975): 'Comment.' In Harold F. Williamson (ed.), *Evolution of International Management Structures*, Newark: University of Delaware Press, 217–24.

Williamson, Harold F. (ed.) (1975): *Evolution of International Management Structures*. Newark: University of Delaware Press.

Williamson, Oliver E. (1967): 'Hierarchical control and optimum firm size.' *Journal of Political Economy*, April, 123–38.

Williamson, Oliver E. (1971): 'The vertical integration of production: market failure considerations.' *American Economic Review*, May, 112–23.

Williamson, Oliver E. (1973): 'Markets and hierarchies: some elementary considerations.' *American Economic Review*, May, 316–25.

Williamson, Oliver E. (1975): *Markets and Hierarchies*. New York: Free Press.

Williamson, Oliver E. (1979): 'Transaction-cost economics: the governance of contractual relations.' *Journal of Law and Economics*, October, 233–61.

Willman, Paul (1982): 'Opportunism in labor contracting.' *Journal of Economic Behavior and Organization*, March, 83–98.

Wilson, Charles (1957): 'The entrepreneur in the industrial revolution in Britain.' *History*, June, 101–17.

Wilson, Charles (1975): 'Multinationals, management and world markets: a historical view.' In Harold F. Williamson (ed.), *Evolution of International Management Structures*, Newark: University of Delaware Press, 193–216.

Wilson, James A. (1980): 'Adaptations to uncertainty and small numbers exchange: the New England fresh fish market.' *Bell Journal of Economics*, Autumn, 491–504.

Wilson, John W. (1975): 'Market structure and interfirm integration in the petroleum industry.' *Journal of Economic Issues*, June, 319–25.

Wolfson, Murray (1966): *A Reappraisal of Marxian Economics*. New York: Columbia University Press.

Woodhouse, W.J. (1938): *Solon the Liberator: A Study of the Agrarian Problem of the Seventh Century*. London: Oxford University Press.

Wright, Gavin (1976): 'Property, progress, and American slavery.' In Paul A. David et al. (eds), *Reckoning With Slavery*, New York: Oxford University Press, 302–36.

Wright, Gavin (1978): *The Political Economy of the Cotton South*. New York: Norton.

Wu, Yuan-Li (1965): *The Steel Industry of Communist China*. New York: Praeger for the Hoover Institution.

Yeo, Cedric A. (1948): 'The overgrazing of ranch-lands in Ancient Italy.' *Transactions and Proceedings of the American Philological Society*, LXXIX, 275–307.

Yeo, Cedric A. (1952): 'The development of the Roman plantation and marketing of farm products.' *Finanzarchiv*, XIII, 321–42.

Yoshino, M.Y. (1971): *The Japanese Marketing System: Adaptations and Innovations*. Cambridge, Mass.: M.I.T. Press.

Zaleski, Eugène (1980): *Stalinist Planning for Economic Growth, 1933–1952*. Chapel Hill: University of North Carolina Press.

Zytkowicz, Leonid (1963): 'An investigation into agricultural production in Masovia in the first half of the 17th century.' *Acta Poloniae Historica*, 18, 99–118.

Index

Aachen 38, 98
Abernathy, William J. 5
acquisition 16, 17
Adelman, Morris 12
Adelmann, Gerhard 99
Adler, F. Michael 8
Aduddell, Robert M. 28, 54
Afghanistan 43
Africa 75, 81
Agmon, Tamir 71
Alchian, Armen A. 19, 24, 115, 154
Allen, Bruce T. 123, 129
Allen, G.C. 43, 73, 74, 75
Allvine, Fred G. 116
Alston, Lee J. 109
Aluminum Company of America 124–9
America, *see* United States
American Can 117
American Tobacco 30, 133
Amsden, Alice H. 79
Anaconda Copper 57
Antwerp 101
Argentina 37, 121
Armour, Henry Ogden 46, 64, 65
Arrow, Kenneth J. 11, 12, 16, 18, 144
Arthur, Henry B. 77
Austen, Ralph 79
Auster, Richard 16, 65, 94, 112, 141, 142, 145, 152, 153

Australia 21, 109
Austrian theory 1
authority 15, 19, 80, 143–4
Averitt, Robert 65

Badische 32
Bailey, Elizabeth E. 65
Bain, Joe S. 43
Baltimore Company 40
bankruptcy potential 15
Baranson, Jack 121
Barkhausen, Max 38
Barzel, Yoram 113
Bauer, P.T. 75
Baumol, William J. 7
Bauwens, L. 31
Beckford, George L. 72
Beckmann, Martin J. 142
Bell Telephone 116
Berend, I.T. 133
Berliner, Joseph S. 119
Berry, M.J. 120
Bessemer, Henry 31–2
Bethlehem Iron 41
Beveridge, Andrew W. 4
Bhatt, V.V. 7
Birmingham 99
Bishop, C.E. 29
Blair, Roger 12
Bloch, Herbert 43
Blum, Jerome 91
Boeing Aircraft 113
Bogue, Allan G. 3, 90

Bohemia 100
Booker, Josias 71
Boston Associates 39, 56
Boston Consulting Group 50
Boston Manufacturing
    Company 39
Boulton, Matthew 55
bounded rationality 50
Bowden, W.H. 71
Boyle, Stanley E. 24, 59, 64, 67
Braun, Rudolf 3
Brazil 36, 37, 40, 56, 57, 76, 121
Brenner, Robert 87, 92
Brimmer, Andrew F. 39, 43
British American Tobacco
    Company 73
British Guiana 71
Brittany 99
Broke, Jean Boine 38
Brooks, R. Charles 29
Brown, Moses 39
Buchanan, Daniel H. 39, 97, 113
Buchanan, James M. 1
Buckley, Peter J. 4, 12, 42
Burbach, Roger 72
Buttrick, John 102

Cain, Louis P. 28, 54
California 33
Calvo, Guillermo A. 153
Camacho, Antonio 143
Campania 82
Canes, Michael E. 65
capitalism 1, 2, 17, 41, 55, 61, 83, 100
Carlton, Dennis W. 18
Carnegie, Andrew 27, 59
Carr, Charles C. 124, 127, 128
Carus-Wilson, Eleanora 101
case studies xi
Casson, Mark 1, 7, 12, 18, 112
Celanese Corporation 61

Central America 77, 113
Chandler, Alfred D. Jr. 6, 23, 30, 32, 46, 63, 133
Channon, Derek F. 72
Chao, Kang 91, 92
Chapman, Stanley D. 55
Chazeau, Melvin G. de 25, 26, 55, 66
Chicago 28, 42, 90
China 37, 73, 74, 114, 120
Christiansen, Robert 75
Chrysler 59, 64
Clark, M. Gardner 120
Cleveland 25
Coase, R.H. 6, 11, 16, 17, 154, 155
code 2, 5
Cohen, Benjamin I. 50, 51
Cohn, David L. 88
Coleman, D.C. 18, 61, 99
Collins, Norman 29
Cologne 98
Columbia 48, 76, 77, 113
communication cost 15–16
conglomerate diversification 22, 131, 136
contracts 11, 14, 15, 23–4, 29, 58, 72–3, 79, 108–9, 113, 116
control loss 153
Corden, W.M. 116
Corey, E. Raymond 127
Courtaulds 61
Cramer, Curtis A. 116
Crawford, Robert G. 24, 115
Crossley, D.W. 43
Crowell, Henry P. 30
Czechoslovakia 118

Dahmén, Erik 35, 54
Danhof, Clarence H. 112
Dannhaeuser, Norbert 74, 110
Davis, Hiram S. 24
Dayan, D. 116

Index

Dean, Warren 37
Deering Harvester Company 27
Del Monte Corporation 72, 77
Demsetz, H. 18
Denmark 42
depletion allowance 116–7
development blocks 35
de Vries, Jan 99
Dhondt, J. 31
Didrichsen, Jon 19, 113
DiPierro, Alberto 1
divestiture 26, 52
Dominican Republic 77
Donkin, R.A. 113
Donnithorne, Audrey G. 43, 73, 74, 75, 121
Dos Santos, Theotonil 179
Dudley, Leonard 48
Duke, James B. 30
Dunning, John H. 6, 8
DuPlessis, Robert S. 99, 100, 101
DuPont 46, 132
Durant, William C. 23

East India Company 40
East Indian Archipelago 36
Eastman, George 30
econometrics xi
economic development 1, 14, 21, 34, 42, 78, 79
economic disturbances 20
economies of scale 85–6, 91, 97, 131
economies of scope 44, 131, 132
Ecuador 77
Edwards, Ronald S. 32, 33, 60
Ellis, Frank 77
employer–employee relationship 15
Engels, Friedrich 139
Engerman, S.L. 97
England, *see* Great Britain

entrepreneurship
   opportunity for 2–5
   role of 1–2
   and urbanization 5
Erickson, Charlotte 3
Erlich, Alexander 119
Etgar, Michael 12, 134
explaining 14–16
exploitation of labor 2, 140, 144

Faler, Paul G. 102
family 2–4, 35, 36, 47
Farnie, D.A. 54, 60
Fenoaltea, Stefano 80, 85
Feuerwerker, Albert 114
Finley, Moses 93
Fisher Body 23, 24, 108, 110
Fite, Gilbert C. 90, 97
Flaherty, M. Therese 11
Flinn, M.W. 113
Florence 99, 114
Flynn, Patricia 72
Fogel, R.W. 97
Fong, Pang Eng 78
Ford 50, 59, 63, 64, 107, 118
France 21, 38, 61
Frederiksen, Martin W. 92, 93
French, A. 93, 94
Freudenberger, Herman 98, 101
Frick, Henry C. 27
Friedlaender, Ann F. 65
Friedman, Milton 147, 148, 153
Friedrichs, Christopher R. 99
Fritz, Kurt von 94
Fugger, family 38
Funk, Isaac 90
futures market 12

Garnsey, Peter 83
Gates, Paul Wallace 89, 93, 94
Gdansk 85, 86

General Foods   117
General Motors   23, 24, 46, 59, 63, 64, 107, 108, 110, 133
Germany   3, 22, 34, 35, 41, 42, 43, 52, 56, 66, 82, 85–7, 99, 132
Gerschenkron, Alexander   34
Ghent   31
Giannola, Adriano   62
Gibbs, George Sweet   18
Gilbert, Charles   28, 39
Goldberg, Victor P.   18
Gort, Michael   20, 21, 66
Gott, Benjamin   39
Goudie, A.W.   22
Graaf, J. de V.   147, 154
Grace, W.R.   4
Graham, Daniel A.   130
Grand Tour   3
Granick, David   62, 118
Great Britain   4, 21, 32, 34, 38, 39, 41, 52, 55, 59, 60, 61, 62, 72, 77, 80, 89, 99, 100, 112, 113, 114, 120, 131
Greece   4, 84
Green, Jerry R.   117
Greenhill, Robert   76
Gregory, Frances W.   2
Guatemala   77
Guffey Petroleum   26

Habakkuk, H.J.   55, 62
Haber, L.F.   32
Hacker, Louis M.   27
Haigh, Robert W.   25, 54, 55, 115, 132
Hale, H.E.   19
Hale, Rosemary D.   19, 126
Halphen, L.   38
Hamilton, F.E. Ian   5, 6
Hamilton, Henry   99, 132
Haniel, Franz   41
Hannah, Leslie   59
Harman, Alvin J.   58

Harris, John R.   7
Hatcher, John   80, 81, 91
Hay, Donald A.   130
Heady, Earl O.   147
Heaton, Herbert   39, 114
Hébert, Robert F.   7
Hennart, Jean-François   19, 47
Herfindahl, Orris C.   57
Higgs, Robert   5, 109
Hill, Hal   74
Hirsch, Seev   71
Hirschmeier, Johannes   36
Hirschleifer, J.   18
Hitachi   34
Hofberr-Schrantz   132
Holesovsky, Vaclav   119
Holloway, Thomas H.   76
Honduras   77
Hopkins, A.G.   75
Hopkins, Keith   82
Howell, Martha C.   99, 100, 101
Hughes, Alan   22
Hungary   118, 132
Hunt, Alfred   41

Illinois   90
Imperial Chemical Industries   4, 61
India   4, 36, 39, 82, 97, 112
industrial revolution   3, 5, 13, 41, 55–6, 61
information
  channel   2, 4, 5
  defined   18
  differentials   12–13
  impactedness   14
  sale of   12
internal organization   15, 107
International Business Machines   58
Ireland   79
Irwin, Manley R.   116
Ishihara, Takemasa   102
Italy   38, 61, 62, 82, 85, 101

Index

Japan 11, 12, 33, 35, 36, 42, 47, 59, 63, 66, 102
Jaspar, Norman 154
Jaynes, Gerald David 94
Jeannin, Pierre 38
Jeffreys, James B. 40
Jensen, William C. 18
Jeremy, David J. 113
Jewkes, John 12
Johnson, Arthur M. 25, 26
Johnson, D. Gale 154
Johnson, Keach 40
Jones, E.L. 52
Jones, Lawrence A. 2, 13, 29
Jones, S.R.H. 114
Joskow, Paul L. 28

Kahn, Alfred K. 25, 26, 55, 66
Kaiser Aluminum 128
Kaldor, N. 50, 147
Kamerschen, David R. 123, 124
Kamiński, Andrzej 85
Kansas 30
Karcz, Jerzy F. 118
Kaserman, David L. 6, 12, 130
Keller, Morton 28
Kennecott Copper 57
Kerridge, Eric 80
Kidron, Michael 43
Kihlstrom, Richard E. 18
Kirkland, Edward C. 97
Kirzner, Israel 1, 6, 7, 142
Klein, Benjamin 24, 115
Klepper, Steven 66
Klíma, Arnošt 95, 100
Knight, Frank H. 17
Knowles, Dom David 80
Kocka, Jürgen 3, 34, 35, 41, 43, 46, 56
Kodak 30, 58, 63
Krooss, Herman E. 28, 39
Krupp, Friedrich 41
Kula, Witold 87, 95, 96
Kydd, Jonathan 75

Laffont, Jean-Jacques 18
Lall, Sanjaya 12, 65, 66
Lancashire 5, 6, 60, 61, 100
Landes, David S. 38
Lane, Frederic Chapin 40
Lazonick, William 61, 62, 145
learning 15–16, 48, 50, 51, 52, 79, 83–4
Lebanon 4
Leff, Nathaniel 36
Leibenstein, Harvey 6
Leiden 100
Lemelin, André 111
Lever Brothers 41
Levin, Richard C. 51, 52, 117, 130
Lévy, Jean-Phillipe 92
Libby, McNeill, and Libby 117
Liggett and Myers 133
Lille 100, 101
Lim, Linda Y.C. 78
Lincolnshire 99
Lipton, Thomas 41
Lis, Catherine 38
Littler, Craig 67
Liverpool 5, 90
Livesay, Harold C. 28, 29, 30, 41
Livingston, S. Morris 115
location problem 5
Lockwood, William W. 35
London 43, 80
Low Countries 38, 80, 99, 101
Lowell, Francis C. 39
Lye, Stephen 136
Lynn 102
Lyon 38

Maarek, Gerald 139, 145
McAleese, Dermot 79
McBride, Mark Edward 122
McCarthy, James L. 57
McDonald, Donogh 79

McGowan, John J.   21, 123
McKee, Robert E.   116
McKie, James W.   117
McLean, John G.   25, 54, 55, 115, 132
McQueen, Matthew   8, 79
Maczak, Anton   86, 95
Maddigan, Ruth J.   58
Magee, Stephen P.   17
Makkai, Laszló   95
Malawi   75, 76
Malaysia   77, 110
Malmgren, H.B.   2, 65
Malowist, Marian   95
managing agency system   36
Manchester   53
Mancke, Richard B.   60
Marglin, Stephen A.   143, 144
market channel development   74
market failure   15
Markham, Jesse W.   61
Marshak, Jacob   153
Marshall, Alfred   153, 155
Martin, D.D.   58
Martin, J. Rod   30
Marx, Karl   1, 92, 139–45
Matarazzo, Francesco   36–7
Matsushita Electric Industrial Company   33
Maxcy, G.   32
May, Stacy   77, 113
Mayhew, Alan   42, 86, 95
Meckling, William H.   18
Meeks, G.   22
Mexico   72, 73
Mezzogiorno   62
Mighell, Ronald L.   2, 13, 29
Mill, John Stuart   145
Miller, Edward   80, 81, 91
Millward, R.   86, 87, 88, 91, 95, 96, 98, 99, 100
Mirrlees, James A.   153
Mitsubishi Company   35

Mitsui Company   35, 36
Mond, Ludwig   4
monopoly   31
  over means of production   143
Monteverde, Kirk   59, 63, 67, 107, 108, 110, 111
Morris, Derek J.   130
Morris Motors   32–3, 59
Mueller, Dennis C.   17, 18
Mueller, Willard F.   29
multinational firm   4, 19
Myrdal, Gunnar   79

Nafziger, E. Wayne   4
Navin, Thomas R.   56
Needham, Douglas   130
Nelson, Daniel   102, 132
Nelson, Ralph L.   21
Nelson, Richard R.   66
Neu, Irene D.   2
Newbury, Colin W.   75
New England   102, 109
New Mexico   30
new product
  defined   13
  income elastic   4
Nichtweiss, Johannes   86, 95
Nigeria   4
Nissan Motor Company   33
North, Douglass C.   144
Norwich   38, 100

Oberschall, Anthony   4
Oklahoma   30
Oliver, Henry Edmund   94

Pakistan   3, 4, 40, 43
Panama   77
Panzar, John C.   136
Papenek, Gustav F.   3, 40, 43
Parker, J.E.S.   52
Parsis   40
Patterson, James M.   116

Index

Pavlovsky, George   42
Peck, Merton J.   123, 124, 128
Peltzman, Sam   122
Pennsylvania   25
Penrose, Edith Tilton   66
Perkins, Edwin J.   2
Perkins, J.A.   53
Perry, Martin K.   125, 126, 127, 128, 136
Petit, Paul   83
Phelps Dodge   57
Philippines   4, 73, 110
Phillips Petroleum   26
Phillips, W.G.   27
pipelines   108, 115–16
Plaza, Galo   77, 113
Poland   85
Polaroid   58
Porter, Glenn   28, 29, 30, 41
Porter, M.E.   130
Postan, M.M.   86
Potter, T.W.   92, 93
Prescott, Edward C.   19
price regulation   115–17
profit   51–2, 130, 143, 144, 149
putting-out system   3, 114

Radner, Roy   153
Rae, John B.   5, 33, 43
Ranki, G.   133
Rathbone, D.W.   82, 83, 92
Ravenscraft, David J.   66
Rawski, Thomas G.   120
Redlich, Fritz   98, 101
regional specialization   5–6
Remington, E.   132
Reynolds Aluminum   128
Rhineland   3, 99
Rhône-Poulenc   61
Rice, Patricia L.   130
Richardson, G.B.   7, 14, 18, 34
risk   14, 136, 149
Robert, Joseph C.   94, 97
Roberts, Brian R.   4, 42

Robinson, E.A.G.   50
Robinson, Joan   133, 146
Rockefeller, John D.   25
Rodrik, Dani   109
Roemer, John   92, 144, 145
Rome   43
Roover, Raymond de   98, 114
Rosen, Sherwin   153
Rosenberg, Nathan   5, 47, 65, 67
routinization   48
Roy, Ewell Paul   29
Royal Dutch Shell   4, 26
Rubin, Paul H.   66
Russia   42, 62, 118, 119

Safford, Frank R.   76
Saham, Junid   78
Samuels, Marcus   4
Schaeffer, Donald   97
Schmalensee, Richard   130
Schmid, A. Allan   145
Schmitt, Hans A.   2
Schmitz, Mark   97
Schrader, Lee F.   29
Schumpeter, Joseph A.   1, 6, 14, 17
Schurmann, Franz   120
Seagraves, J.A.   29
secrecy   17, 39
Semple, Ellen Churchill   94
serfdom   81, 92, 96
sharecropping   84, 91, 94, 150
Sheffield   31
shirking   16, 17, 47, 53, 83, 89, 94, 96, 97, 114, 141, 142, 148, 149, 153
Silbertson, Aubrey   136
Silesia   3, 99
Silver, Morris   16, 18, 65, 94, 112, 139, 142, 145, 152, 153
Simon, Herbert A.   15, 50
Singapore   51, 78
Singh, Ajit   22

Slater, Samuel   39
slavery   82, 89
Smith, Adam   131
Snia Viscosa   61
sogo shosha   11
Soly, Hugo   38
South Korea   51, 77
Soviet Union, *see* Russia
Spence, A.M.   130
Stalin, Joseph V.   118
Standard Fruit Company   77
Standard Oil Company   25, 26, 54
Starr, Chester G.   94
Stein, Stanley J.   56
Stigler, George   117, 131, 135
Strassman, W. Paul   56, 61
Supreme Court   26
Sussex   43
Sweden   35, 42, 54
Swift Company   28, 54

Taiwan   51, 79
Tamura, Masorori   34
Tate and Lyle   72
team   153
Teece, David J.   6, 46, 59, 63, 64, 65, 67, 107, 108, 110, 111
Texas   26, 30, 90
Textron   133
thangata system
Third World   3
Thirsk, Joan   8
Thoburn, J.T.   78, 79
Tilly, Richard   21, 22, 66
Tokyo   33
Topolski, Jerzy   87, 88, 95
Toshiba Company   33
tourism   8
Townsend, Harry   32, 33
transfer pricing   116–17
Tucker, Irwin B.   135, 137
Type I error   xi–xii

uncertainty, defined   18
Unger, Richard W.   40
United Africa Company   75
United Engineers   78
United Fruit   96
United Kingdom, *see* Great Britain
United Societies   132
United States   2, 5, 21, 28, 33, 37, 39, 41, 56, 59, 61, 62, 64, 76, 88, 90, 112, 117, 120, 134
universalism   62

Van Werveke, H.   38, 101
Venice   40
Vernon, John M.   130
Vernon, Raymond   4, 5, 8
vertical integration
   defined   11
   measurement of   134
visible hand   6, 63
Visscher, Michael   19

Waldman, Don E.   117, 122
Wallace, Donald H.   126
Walsh, Margaret   28
Ware, Caroline F.   39, 56
Warren-Boulton, Frederick   130
Waswo, Ann   42, 66
Waterson, Michael   130
wealth, personal   2, 83–4
Wedgwood, Josiah   55
Wellisz, Stanislaw   153
Westfield, Fred M.   130
West Indies   72
Weston, J. Fred   147
Westphalia   3, 99
White Consolidated Industries   133
White, K.D.   92, 93, 94
White, William D.   143
Wilder, Donald P.   135, 137

Wilkins, Mira 8, 30
Williamson, Oliver E. 6, 14, 18, 46, 108, 153, 154
Willig, Robert R. 136
Willman, Paul 109
Wilson, Charles 4, 13, 21, 37, 41, 99, 114
Wilson, James A. 109
Winter, Sydney 66
Wisconsin 29
Woodhouse, W.J. 84
Wright, Gavin 89, 96, 97
Wu, Yuan-Li 120

Xerox 58

Yataro, Iwasaki 35
Yeo, Cedric A. 82, 92, 93
Yokohama 33
Yorkshire 38, 99, 114
Yui, Tsunehiko 36

zaibatsu
Zaleski, Eugène 119
Zambia 4
Zurich 3
Zusman, Pinhas 12
Zytkowicz, Leonid 95